FRANCHISING FROM THE INSIDE OUT

FRANCHISING FROM THE INSIDE OUT

Ed Teixeira

To order additional copies of this book, contact:
Xlibris Corporation
1-888-795-4274
www.Xlibris.com
Orders@Xlibris.com
27244

CONTENTS

To my wife, Carol, son, Eddie, and daughter, Denise,
for their love and support.

My mother, Dorothy Teixeira, and my late father, Edward
Teixeira, one of the members of the "greatest generation,"
who gave me a thirst for knowledge and taught me that
success can come to all who strive for it.

ACKNOWLEDGMENTS

Although I considered writing a book about franchising for the past several years, it required the encouragement and support of two important people.

My wife, Carol, who helped to edit this book and has provided me unwavering support and encouragement throughout my entire business career, which at times caused her to sacrifice her own career aspirations; and my former administrative assistant and friend, Kathy LoFrese, who not only typed most of this book, but continued to "push" me when I would lapse into periods of inactivity. Kathy has my sincere gratitude and appreciation for all of her help.

I also wish to thank the many attorneys, franchisors, and franchisees who assisted in the writing of this book by contributing their time, knowledge, and experiences.

I thank Craig Tractenberg, a well-respected franchise attorney and friend, who took the time out of a very busy schedule to offer his objective comments on the contents of this book.

INTRODUCTION

During a United States Department of Commerce-sponsored trade mission to Europe a number of years ago, which included franchisors and consultants, the leader of the trade mission, *Andy Kostecka* of the Department of Commerce and the originator of "Franchising in the Economy," told me that the most effective franchise consultants are those individuals who had worked for franchisors in "operations." Then, looking directly at me, he said, "People like you, who have worked in every area of franchising." I have never forgotten those words and as a franchise "insider" I want to share this knowledge about franchising. Throughout my career of over twenty five years my insight into franchising has evolved into an understanding which can benefit both franchisees and franchisors.

This book is a culmination of my dream to share this insight with prospective franchisees and franchisors. People who see the great opportunity that franchising can provide, yet recognize the risks that exist.

I've been fortunate to spend the majority of my business career in the franchising industry. Franchisors that I have worked with have run the gamut from the franchise builders who grew their company from the ground up to corporate leaders who converted their existing business into a franchise company.

Prior to working in the franchise industry, I had worked for a Fortune 500 retailer. The immediate difference that I noted between the corporate and franchise model was that in the franchise company independent owners operated their own business. Although my prior experience was with companies run by corporate employees, my introduction to franchising was, as they say, "love at first sight." I related to the concept of franchising immediately and found the process refreshing and exciting. I have been pleased to have made the choice back then and continue to be impressed by the growth and vibrancy of the franchise industry.

I have had experience selling franchises, writing franchise agreements, supporting franchise networks, and establishing franchise advisory councils. I have witnessed numerous franchisees achieve financial rewards beyond their wildest dreams. On the other hand, I have seen the other side of franchising, which includes franchisor-franchisee litigation, the franchisor shifting emphasis from a franchise to a company-owned network and franchisees losing their investment and more. I have seen franchisees, which on a comparative financial basis were more successful than the franchisor. I've also been a franchisee, which gave me the real-life experience of having "walked in the shoes" of a franchisee.

It's because of my franchise resume and my fondness for the concept of franchising that I find it particularly rewarding to share my experience with others.

I have organized this book in such a way as to provide meaningful information for future and existing franchisees as well as for franchisors. I'll present the key aspects of franchising that influence prospective and existing franchisees. You will learn about franchising from someone who has spent the majority of his business career as a franchise executive. My intent is to give you a thorough understanding of franchising which will include information and insight that new franchisees and new franchisors may not possess.

You will understand the thought process of franchisors and why they put certain provisions in the franchise agreement. This is not an exposé on franchising, but rather a compendium of information for franchisees from a franchisor perspective.

It's important to keep in mind that both the franchisor and franchisee are in business to earn a profit. This is not meant to insult the reader's intelligence, but rather to have this fact serve as a constant reminder that the fundamental basis of the relationship between the franchisor and franchisee is based upon a financial bond. Issues and topics that you will read about in this book typically have franchisor and/or franchisee profitability as a basis.

This doesn't mean that the franchise relationship is cold and somehow lacks a human side. In fact, I can truthfully say that I have enjoyed an enormous amount of personal satisfaction from the many relationships and successes of the countless franchisees that I have met. However, one must always remember that most decisions made by both franchisor and franchisees are financial in nature. I never met a franchisee or franchisor that went into business to lose money.

There is another component to this relationship that is linked to the financial issue and that is growth. Growth in business, be it number of outlets, sales volume, or product sales, is a driver of profitability. Franchisees must keep this fact in mind when they request a larger territory as part of his/her franchise. Franchisors will often ask the question, "Can that franchisee grow the territory?" The foundation of a franchisor business model typically relies upon increased growth. If you go into a franchise system thinking you will be the only "show in town," think again. Of course, if you have millions of dollars to invest in a high-end restaurant or hotel franchise, you can enjoy a good degree of independence in your territory.

My expectation is to provide a backdrop of information so that potential or existing franchisees will be able to understand and perhaps even think like a franchisor and vice versa.

I've organized this book in such a way that a prospective franchisee can follow those steps which will hopefully lead to the best possible opportunity for success. When meeting prospective franchisees, I would tell them that the franchising process is important for the franchise candidate. To emphasize this point, I would remind them that it's far easier for a franchisor to recover from the mistake of choosing the wrong franchisee than it is for a franchisee to recover from choosing the wrong franchisor.

As we all know, there are no guarantees in life. However, you can minimize the risks that you face when choosing and opening a new franchise. I established a format for you to follow so that if you decide that franchising is an area that you would like to pursue, you'll have a roadmap to follow. You will have a method for finding the franchise that will best fit your attributes, your capital, and your aspirations.

From a legal standpoint, I have seen attorneys, who were representing franchisees negotiate components or provisions in franchise agreements that were of little value, when compared to other more important provisions. Although, this may be the result of a lack of franchise experience on the part of some attorneys, it confirms the fact that there must be a basic understanding of franchising when people review franchise agreements. An attorney who does not understand franchising may not know what to focus on and what points are important. Also, they may not understand the reasons why many franchise provisions are written the way they are.

You will gain insight regarding how to validate and evaluate the franchisor. Can the franchisor provide you the services in the territory within which you will operate your franchise? Are they committed to the success of their franchisees? Also, you will be able to benefit from my experience in designing and constructing franchise agreements and administering franchise networks as well as in negotiating and dealing with disputes that have arisen between franchisees and franchisors.

I will present the kinds of questions you should be asking the franchisor which most franchisees may not even think of asking. Once again, you will have the benefit of my experience from a franchisors perspective in knowing what you should look for when you evaluate the franchisor.

I'll teach you to understand the complete "franchisee package" and not just what might seem to be an exciting franchise opportunity. You'll also have the comfort of knowing if the franchisor is providing the support they promised.

I will advise you how to negotiate with the franchisor and what I consider to be the so-called "non-negotiable items" in the franchise agreement. Those areas that franchisors typically will not negotiate. You'll learn how they can grant certain concessions in negotiating, when in fact they are really not giving up very much.

One point I want to emphasize is that there is no perfect franchise. One should remember that even within some of the best franchise programs, there are franchisees that fail. On the other hand, I have seen franchisees that have operated within programs that have not been the strongest, yet these franchisees were extremely successful. It goes without saying that the two most important ingredients in this relationship are the franchisor and the franchisee. That's assuming that the franchise itself, the products or the services that are part of the franchise, are viable and in demand. If you were to read some of the literature on franchising, you would see certain questions that prospective franchisees are encouraged to ask the franchisor. These questions will usually deal with the type of franchise, what are the long-term trends and are the products or services valuable and in demand?

Since success is often duplicated many times over you should always remember that what today might seem like the "hot" franchise will probably be duplicated in some manner in the months and years to follow.

I will guide the readers of this book on a journey from the start of a franchise search to signing the franchise agreement and ultimately becoming a franchisee. I have included advice and information for franchisees in terms of how to deal with certain issues and how to understand the process of dispute resolution, if unfortunately, a problem arises.

One of the misconceptions that I have observed over the many years is that franchisees do not understand how much power they really have, and quite frankly, I have seen many franchisees accept what I would consider to be subpar performance on the part of the franchisor. The franchisee may be unwilling, based upon a lack of understanding, to challenge the franchisor. In some cases, this could be the result of a fear of retribution; in other cases it could be the case of not fully understanding their franchisee rights. As a signatory to a franchise agreement, the franchisee is entitled to hold the franchisor responsible for the services that the franchisor is obligated to provide its franchisee.

I recall among my responsibilities as a regional director was to schedule weekly newspaper advertising on behalf of my twenty-eight franchisees. My initial goal was to develop a consensus among my franchisees regarding advertised specials. I soon became aware of the fact that when you design an ad and seek input from different people, you'll get as many different opinions as the number of people you ask. During one of these meetings, I was approached by my largest franchisee that took me aside. His message was simple and I quote, "You should make the decision based on input from some of your reliable franchisees. If you don't do it this way, you'll never get anything done." I never forgot that advice. Throughout my franchise career, I followed the practice of gathering input from a select group of successful franchisees and then announcing my decision based upon that input. I believe that many franchisors follow this practice.

If this book can help just a few franchisees make the right choices, I will have reached my objective. For franchisors, I'll offer insight into what I consider to be the formula for success. I've worked with franchise networks where the franchisor was financially successful out of proportion to the franchisees. On the other hand, I've been a part of a franchise network where the franchisor was marginally profitable. I devote several chapters to franchisors using my experience in having dealt with hundreds of franchise issues.

Finally, there is one category of information you won't find in this book and that is information pertaining to specific franchisors (except in the few instances when I use certain franchisors to demonstrate a point). The reason for this is twofold:

1. Much of the franchise information is dated and as such can change from the time I included it to the time someone may have read the book.
2. In today's ever-changing business environment, companies can undergo changes that can swing from successful organization to failed company.

For these reasons I don't feel it appropriate to reference other franchise companies.

I hope you enjoy this book and find the small investment worthwhile.

CHAPTER 1

Franchise History

According to PriceWaterhouseCoopers there
were 767,483 establishments in franchise systems
in the United States in 2001 which provided
9,797,117 direct jobs.

Obviously, you have an interest in franchising or already work in the industry; otherwise, you probably wouldn't have bought this book, unless you happen to be a business historian. Before we embark on a journey of finding the right franchise for you, assuming of course this is the business that you want to enter, I think it's important that you have a background and understanding about franchising and how it has grown into such a dynamic industry.

The International Franchise Association estimates that American consumers spend approximately 1.3 trillion dollars on franchise goods and services on an annual basis. As far back as the nineteenth century, oil companies and other manufacturing giants granted franchises to businesses. Although not specifically called franchises, these entities granted rights to distribute their products. Examples of this could be as simple as a monopoly to companies that operated utilities in our cities or a distributorship for automobiles. These early beginnings of franchising are far removed from what we see in today's modern world.

The franchise that I grew up with as a very young boy and one that became an American institution was Howard Johnson. Howard Johnson began in 1925 as a very small ice cream shop that evolved from what we would consider to be a drug store. The store sold three flavors of ice cream and the founder, a 27-year-old from Wollaston, Massachusetts, named Howard Johnson, thought that he could expand the different flavors of ice cream, and hopefully, improve the quality of the product he was selling.

Before long, Johnson added hotdogs and hamburgers and some other foods to the point that what began as his little store evolved into a restaurant. He recognized that this was a future for him to pursue. He opened up another restaurant in 1929 and then a few years later, considered the concept of franchising. Howard Johnson contacted a businessman about placing the Howard Johnson name on his restaurant on Cape Cod. The agreement was that there would be a fee for the use of the Howard Johnson name and an agreement that the restaurant owner would buy certain foods and supplies from Johnson.

The program worked very well for both people and Johnson began to make similar agreements with others. That was the beginning of restaurant franchising and would evolve, obviously, into so many other products and businesses throughout the country, but most important, it was the beginning of the restaurant franchise industry.

Of course, the most well-known restaurant franchise in the world is McDonalds. So much has been written about Ray Crock and the McDonalds' brothers that McDonalds and Crock have become an institution. The first McDonalds was opened in Des Plaines, Illinois, in 1955 and soon afterward, more McDonalds outlets continued to open. Today, there are more than 30,000

McDonalds in 118 countries. There is no doubt that when it comes to franchising and fast foods in general, McDonalds is the leader of the pack.

During the 1960s and early 1970s, franchising continued to gain in appeal with a number of companies joining the world of franchising. I lived in Louisville, Kentucky, in the early 1980s where franchising had spawned many companies, not the least of which was the famous Kentucky Fried Chicken franchise. Having encountered people who knew individuals who had been in this franchise in the 1960s or 1970s, I recall a story of one young man who went home and told his parents that he was going to Texas to do something new: sell KFC franchises. Some of these people, like this young man, would ultimately become millionaires based upon the success and growth of what they did. Many of them ultimately ended up owning KFCs.

In the environment of the 1960s and 1970s, the growth of the franchise industry exploded. However, like comparable situations, which involve an industry experiencing dynamic growth, this growth can attract unsavory individuals and companies. During this period of rapid franchise growth, there were companies that were unscrupulous. There were fraudulent franchisors that took money from honest people who either failed to produce or were undercapitalized. As a result, they were not able to provide the services they promised. Many of them went bankrupt and this left their franchisees, which in many cases had invested their life savings, without anywhere to turn, other than the courts.

In response to this climate and the kind of problems that took place within the franchising industry, in 1979 the Federal Trade Commission enacted regulations, which required all franchisors to provide prospective franchisees certain written disclosures. State attorneys general and securities administrators suggested a more manageable form of written disclosure called the Uniform Franchise Offering Circular or UFOC. The UFOC had to be provided to the prospective franchisees before any money could be accepted by the franchisor.

Throughout this book, you will see a number of references to the UFOC (sometimes referred to as the FOC for Franchise Offering Circular; I prefer to use UFOC) and learn how it has evolved into the document that it is today. This document provides the franchise candidate, who is the prospective investor, certain information they need to know in order to make intelligent and accurate decisions about the franchisor and the franchise opportunity.

As you pursue your dream of acquiring a franchise, always be aware of the fact that the UFOC was designed to provide the franchise candidate information that would enable them to make a meaningful decision. Without getting into too much of the legal area, the rule of thumb about the UFOC and the information that it contains is founded upon the concept that certain information impacts the decision that an individual would make, as to whether they would acquire a franchise and as such what ought to be in there.

As I write this book, the FTC recently completed a comprehensive review of the so-called Franchise Rule, which governs the regulatory aspects of franchising and in particular franchise disclosure. One of the recommendations is that there would be a specific regulatory distinction between business format franchises and so-called business opportunities. Another change would be to allow for widespread delivery of the UFOC via electronic transmission or e-mail. There are other changes that the FTC staff recommended which are expected to be implemented. Since these recommendations have yet to be enacted, I will continue to refer to existing franchise disclosure regulations.

As you read and learn more about the UFOC and review the UFOC for specific franchise companies, you will see that there is a format to the information and how it is presented. The reason for this is so that you, as a prospective franchisee, can be provided with the information that you need to make the right decision.

Not everything about the franchisee and franchisor will be included in the UFOC. There may very well be information that will not be in the UFOC or will not be presented in enough detail to help you fully understand what needs to be done in terms of your decision. You'll learn about ways that will enable you to gather additional information about the franchise opportunity you are pursuing.

Now, in addition to franchise companies, there are also what is defined as a "business opportunity." To clarify any misconception or confusion that one may have, a franchise is considered a business opportunity, but a business opportunity is not necessarily a franchise. One of the best examples I can give you of a business opportunity would be those paper "tear off" strips of telephone numbers you see posted at an ATM or telephone booth where you are told to call a certain number and find out how you can earn money.

Business opportunities sometimes do get confused with franchising. There are many business opportunity shows or exhibits around the country. Business opportunities are advertised in newspapers and there is even a magazine devoted to business opportunities.

The typical business opportunity could be working at home on crafts or stuffing envelopes. Installing vending machines or even installing an ATM machine in a certain location is an example of a business opportunity. You need to be very careful about business opportunity offers, such as having the right to sell TV access to the Internet or giving seminars on how to make money on the Internet.

You can assume that there are probably a lot more fraudulent business opportunities than there are fraudulent franchise opportunities. There are statutes on the books of many states as well as the FTC dealing with business opportunities. These statutes include requirements that business opportunities be registered with that particular state. However, you can rest assured that some of them are not registered. The best way to validate a business opportunity is to contact your local state agency or consumers' department to find out whether there have been any complaints or if the business opportunity is registered.

Returning to the area of franchising, however, with the arrival of the franchise rule in 1979, the Federal Trade Commission introduced a common set of guidelines that required all franchisors to provide information on specific areas to prospective franchisees.

I feel it is very important for you to have an understanding of franchising, its origination and its development. Franchising is a powerful business engine that represents a tremendous amount of business activity, not only in the United States but also throughout the world. There are a number of situations where you may wish to pursue more information regarding franchising and if you go to the Internet and the FTC Web site, there is information available that you can look through that will provide you with guidance.

If you have chosen to seek franchising as a way to own and operate your own business in order to be successful and independent, then be sure that you make the right decision for you and the capital you will be investing in this business.

A definition of franchising, which I found quite accurate over the years, is that it is a form of business in which a company with a successful product or service (the franchisor) enters into a continuing contractual relationship with the franchisees using the franchisor's trade name with the franchisor's guidance in exchange for a fee.

One franchisor had a management staff that had no franchise experience at all. Its product was providing healthcare services. Although, the CEO was deeply committed to the franchising concept, the rest of management either didn't agree with franchising in healthcare or those who did immediately thought of fast food whenever they heard the word "franchise." They really didn't understand franchising as a business model, but rather related to franchising from a product standpoint. I became the franchise guru because most of management did not understand that franchising is about relationships. For me, the best part was that I had a great deal of authority with little responsibility.

This is an example where you will find a franchise operating within an environment that is not commonly associated with franchising. In fact, in this particular case, there were very few corporate employees who had any kind of franchise experience at all. Although this is somewhat of an exception, it just goes to prove that franchising can exist and will sometimes work in any business or industry.

Franchising is so pervasive it can be found in virtually every developed country in the world. Moreover, as shown in the appendix, there are Franchise Industry Associations from China to Finland.

Mr. *Eitaro Takahashi*, who works for Saint-Care, a large Japanese franchisor involved in the healthcare industry in Japan, spent two years in the United States learning about franchising. He says, "Franchising in the United States is very dynamic and highly accepted. In Japan, franchising continues to grow in popularity but has not yet reached the same level of acceptance it has in the United States. In the United States the typical franchisee may have a more clearly defined and more independent role than his counterpart in Japan. This difference reflects the maturity of the franchise industry in the United States."

If you are serious about pursuing a franchise business, I think you will have to be prepared to make some decisions regarding how you are organized and with whom you will associate. One of the considerations that you will have to make is related to your business organization or structure. Do you intend to operate this franchise yourself or will you have a partner? I would suggest, unless it is a member of your family, that there is no guarantee that you won't have some problems. Even family members who enter partnerships have problems or issues. I can say that a partnership, unlike a marriage, means that when you have a fight you don't go to bed with your partner. The other observation about a partnership is that when things are going well, partnerships generally work well. It's when there is adversity that affects the business that the relationship gets tested. If you are thinking of acquiring a franchise and within your organizational structure you intend to have a partner, just be advised that whether you operate as a corporation is less of a factor than dealing with a partner in your business. Partnerships can be very difficult and after my last experience, I swore the only partner I'll ever have again is the one I have been married to for thirty-four years.

Although it is not necessary at this time to consider the type of organizational structure that your franchise will take, be advised that in many cases the franchisors will expect you to incorporate. There are various forms of corporations that you could utilize, however, the more preferred is the limited liability company LLC or Sub-S corporation that provide certain tax benefits for small business owners. The more recent limited liability company has advantages that will benefit certain individuals depending upon their needs. It's not necessary that you incorporate before beginning your search for a franchise; however, you ought to be prepared and should have already considered the type of structure that you will have when you are ready to operate your franchise.

Clearly, you should avoid proprietorships since you will have liability as an individual for certain acts that your business may have committed, whether it's a failure to pay bills, etc. The corporate veil is preferred because it can insulate individuals from certain liabilities; however, as you will see later in this book, many franchisors may require a personal guarantee so that if the franchisee, which is a corporation, incurs certain obligations to the franchisor, then the individuals who operate the franchise will guarantee those obligations. I'll deal with this matter in more detail later on in the book. You need to have competent financial and legal counsel to guide you toward making the right decision regarding your business entity.

Is Franchising Right for You?

Before you make the decision to embark on a franchise search, you need to be sure that franchising is the right path for you to follow. Following are some items that should be considered:

Be prepared to give up some business freedom. Although a major benefit of franchising flows from the synergy of its franchisees, the overall success of franchising results from a process or system designed for the franchise operation. If you are a true entrepreneur or highly creative person, then you might find franchising somewhat confining. This is not to say that creativity is not welcome in a franchise operation. However, following the franchise program is the most important aspect of that business. Be reminded that some franchise opportunities by their very nature require conformity and consistency in order to be successful. The food franchise opportunities are an example of this.

You'll be operating under a contract or agreement that you may find very restrictive. Keep in mind that your conduct and behavior as a business owner, in a sense, will be guided by a franchise agreement. This is not to say those franchise agreements are so restrictive that you are not free to do your thing from time-to-time, but rather the overall operation of your business must conform to the requirements of the franchise agreement. In my own personal experience, I've seen some outstanding franchisees become quite frustrated when they had an idea or a concept that they wanted to introduce in their franchise but were prevented from doing so by their franchise agreement. This is a situation where the franchisors are unable to allow the franchisee to stray too far away from the requirements of the agreement since other franchisees could follow suit.

Be prepared for long hours, some disappointment, and some tough challenges. For anyone who has gone from working in the corporate world,

franchising offers some outstanding benefits, not
the least of which is "you are your own boss." Your
success may be related to your own willingness to
work hard. On the other hand, you need to
recognize that once you acquire a franchise, you
are owner as well as boss. With that, comes a
requirement that you're the "go-to person." If you
happen to have been an executive in a company,
you certainly realize that in many cases you were
the key focal point for decision making or the
person that was at the top of the hierarchy
whenever there were problems or issues. This is
the same situation in a franchise, only magnified.
Because you own the business, you are the one
that has to make it work, and although you can
depend upon other people, you have to be the
one that is there when needed. There may also be
situations where things don't work out quite as
well as you thought they would, whether it's
getting off to the right start financially or losing a
key employee which could retard your business
growth. These are the kinds of setbacks that are
normal for any new business and a franchise is not
a guarantee of success. So, it's very important to
be prepared for the fact that you may have some
setbacks. Challenges will certainly arise and these
challenges could be in the form of being required
to invest additional capital in your business, since
it is your business and you're not operating a
publicly traded company.

Your risk of capital is extremely important,
and as such, you need to be very sure of your
decision before you proceed. Once you sign the
franchise agreement, you have signed a contract
and you are required to fulfill the obligations of
that contract. You will be investing your hard-

earned capital and for some of you, it may be everything that you can scrape together. Just be sure that you do the correct due diligence and are confident that the franchise you ultimately choose is one that you can be successful at.

Recognize that you may be dealing with a franchisor staff member who wields a certain amount of authority over you, yet may have far less business experience and accomplishments than you. Keep in mind that many franchisors do have field staff or supervisory staff that they utilize to verify the compliance of the franchisees. These individuals are an important part of franchisor management. If you, in fact, came from a top management level in a company then you may be much more knowledgeable about business than some of the individuals who represent the franchisor. You have to understand this and be willing to work with these individuals. I should point out that most franchisors recognize the need for their staff to have good interpersonal skills and how to conduct themselves in a franchise environment. Therefore, I wouldn't suggest much anxiety on your part over the fact that you may have supervisors with less business savvy or experience than you, but you should be aware of it.

Jeff Bernstein, president and CEO of Trufoods Corp., which operates Arthur Treacher's Fish and Chips, Wall Street Deli, and Pudgies Chicken, states that "we look for franchisees who have business experience not necessarily restaurant related, but who have entrepreneurial personalities." He feels that ambition and the desire to succeed are critical factors in the selection process.

As a final suggestion, if you decide to pursue the franchise and follow the steps that I have set forth, then I think the aforementioned issues or concerns will take care of themselves. If you follow the general guidelines that are set forth in this book, then your opportunity for success will be that much higher and you will be assured that the franchise that you choose is operated by a franchisor that operates in a manner that is compatible to the expectations that you have as a franchisee.

If on the other hand you choose not to pursue a franchise, your only cost has been the price of this book and it may be the best money you ever spend.

CHAPTER 2

Finding the Franchise to Fit Your Needs

How do you choose from over 2,000 franchises?

The International Franchise Association's *Franchise Opportunities Guide* lists more than 1,000 companies that offer franchises. If one were to include other franchise programs that are not listed in the IFA guide, the number would rise to more than 2,000. Obviously, there are countless franchise opportunities available.

Selecting a franchise is only the first step in working through the process of acquiring and joining a franchise program. When considering a franchise opportunity, one must always keep in mind that there are three key factors that should guide your decision.

- First, choosing a business or product that you will feel most confident marketing and operating;
- Second, having the amount of experience that is required to operate the particular type of business you select; and

- Third, having the necessary working capital available to invest in a franchise.

- First, in considering the franchise and the type of product or services that have the greatest appeal, there may be a tendency to choose a franchise that offers a certain amount of sizzle or glamour. Be careful. You want to be sure that the services or products that are part of the franchise are something that you can comfortably market and sell. If your background is in technical services and you feel uncomfortable making "cold calls" trying to generate business, then perhaps a business, which requires direct sales, might not be your best choice. If, however, you have a sales personality and enjoy interacting with people and selling, then you might be better off dealing with a service franchise which require different skills and experience as opposed to a franchise that has a technical component to it, such as a printing franchise or perhaps even a food franchise. Once again, you want to choose a segment of the franchise industry that you feel comfortable with. So, your first approach is to consider those kinds of industries, products or services that provide you this comfort and also that you feel demonstrate an opportunity for growth.

- Second, you want to be sure that you have the prerequisite business experience and skills to be able to operate the franchise. Some franchise programs require very little staff, which means that the franchisee is basically the key operator of the business. There are other franchises that require a good amount of personnel. Some of the temporary employment franchises, although only employing several office people, may deal with virtually hundreds of temporary employees. This requires a certain degree of experience in managing people as well as a comfort level in dealing with various issues be it operating a payroll, billing system, etc.

  Be careful that you don't end up being a "fish out of water" by getting involved with a franchise or a segment of the franchise industry that is foreign to you. This does not alter the fact that many franchises are "cookie-cutter" in design, which means the operation is very structured. Nevertheless, no one can deny the fact that people and management skills are an important component of any business operation no matter how well organized. Also, be aware of the fact that if you don't have the skills to operate the franchise, you may be forced to depend upon someone else. When you rely upon someone else, there could very well be a point in time when this person becomes so important to the business that he or she could figuratively speaking hold you hostage. There are exceptions, such as an absentee owner who might hire a manager to operate a large franchise.

- Third, be sure you have the amount of capital necessary to start up and operate the business. I would always suggest to prospective franchisees that whatever their cash flow model shows, they put in a risk factor of 10 percent or more for unexpected contingencies. I have seen many cash flow statements and pro forma financials that were overly optimistic and didn't allow for a margin of error. In the real world, unanticipated events happen and one must always be prepared for these events. The last thing a franchisee needs is to operate their new franchise for three to six months, only to find that they do not have enough working capital to sustain the growth of the business. Your available working capital will determine the kind of franchise you will be acquiring. Obviously, upscale franchises that require significant amounts of capital are much more complex and also require a much higher level of staff. One can go from a small fast-food format or service franchise that might require two or three employees all the way up to a full-size restaurant or hotel. The difference is not only the size of the business, but the amount of working capital that is required. It has been my experience that people who pursue the larger franchises will employ the appropriate financial advisors, accountants, and attorneys, to make sure that their money is wisely invested. Therefore there is a direct correlation between the size of the investment and the scrutiny a franchise opportunity will undergo.

Once you have a sense as to what your franchise parameters are, then you can begin to look at those franchise opportunities that fit the requirements and guidelines that I've just presented.

There are many resources available for identifying franchise opportunities. There is the IFA *Franchise Opportunities Guide,* which is a directory of more than 1,000 franchise companies. The IFA also schedules franchise expos, which feature franchise opportunities and various educational programs. I would caution you that these franchise shows usually represent a small percent of all of the franchisee opportunities that are available. However, you will still have the opportunity to meet franchisor representatives face-to-face and this can provide you experience. Perhaps, you'll even find one or two franchises that interest you.

If you have a specific franchise in mind, a franchise expo may provide you the opportunity to visit this franchise in person. There are franchise publications such as *Entrepreneur Magazine, Bond's Franchise Guide, The Franchise Handbook,* and others that present franchise opportunities to include descriptions of each franchise. On the Internet, there are many resources such as www.*franchisetrade.com* that can provide information on franchises as well.

In my experience, the best resource for identifying franchise opportunities is the International Franchise Association. It is the largest and oldest franchise trade association in which there are hundreds of franchisors and a large number of franchisee members. The IFA is a good resource for identifying what franchises are available by industry segment, product, or service group. These franchisors are also IFA members. You'll find that the IFA also provides a vast array of information and services to prospective franchisees. The IFA "Franchise Opportunities Guide" lists all of its member franchisors by category with specific information.

Here is some very important advice. I've observed that most prospective franchisees will look through a franchise book, choose a franchise and then proceed to get the details of how the franchise operates, etc. This might even include visits to the prospective franchisors. I recommend that your first step should be to identify the industry segment, service, or product that you are interested in. Select two or three franchises from that family group and then contact each franchisor to get preliminary information.

However, before you go into a great amount of detail, I would suggest you first speak to some of the franchisees. Their names and numbers are in the UFOC. The point being that by speaking to the franchisees first, you will be able to get an indication as to what their experience and results have been with that franchise program.

The sales process that most franchisors follow is to speak to the candidate. Franchisors qualify them in terms of their level of interest, business experience, and available capital. Franchisors then sell the franchise through a consultative process. Within the franchise industry, there are some sales representatives who will aggressively sell a franchise. However, many franchisors will take more of a consultative approach, which means that they will provide the prospective franchisee with the necessary information to help lead that franchisee to the right decision. This is an approach, which I followed throughout my entire career, since I truly felt that one has to provide the franchisee the information that they need in order to make an intelligent decision. Once the franchisor crosses the line and tries to "sell" the franchisee the franchise, then both parties can end up having problems. You have to be cautious as a prospective franchisee to follow a particular process and not allow yourself to be "sold." You must convince yourself rather than let someone else convince you! Be wary of aggressive franchise sales representatives who try to "push" you into a decision or will behave more like a salesperson than a consultant.

The IFA *Franchise Opportunities Guide* contains over seventy-five categories of franchises ranging from accounting to weight control. There is, in fact, a business opportunity to fit virtually

everyone's needs. The January 2004 *Entrepreneur Franchise 500*
listed over 750 franchises of which 335 had less than 100 locations.
Of the remaining franchises, there were 106 with more than 500
locations of which 69 companies had been in business for more
than twenty years. *Entrepreneur Franchise 500* ranks the top 500
using a number of categories.

As you can see, there are a large number of franchises to choose
from and the choice you make could be one of the more important
decisions you'll ever make. I'd like to suggest a format to follow
which will hopefully lead you to select the type of franchise you
should pursue. Although you often hear the term "cookie cutter"
to describe certain franchise programs, there are very few that are
so cookie cutter that they basically can run themselves. Although
most franchise programs do have an operating system, which can
minimize the mistakes and errors in running that business;
nevertheless, there are certain unique attributes to each franchise
and that's what you must focus on rather than believing that the
operating system is designed to be "foolproof."

Following are the key steps to follow:

1. In view of your experience and working capital, eliminate
    those franchises that do not qualify. As an example, if you
    don't have financial experience or training, you can eliminate
    accounting and tax services. If your background and
    experience are nontechnical, you may be quick to eliminate
    automotive services. In terms of working capital, you could
    rule out hotel franchises and high-end restaurants. I suggest
    you utilize *IFA Opportunities Guide*, *Entrepreneur Franchise
    500*, *The Franchise Handbook*, and *Bonds Franchise Guide*
    to review the various categories of franchise opportunities.
    These publications are available at bookstores. Most of
    these listings will show the required investment.

2. Choose franchise categories that appeal to you from a
    product or service standpoint and which are compatible
    with your business background and investment capability.

Keep in mind that you can also use the Internet to do a search as well.

3. Once you narrow your choices down to particular companies, you can use the Internet to review the franchise program since most franchisors have their own Web site. This provides you a way to browse through various franchise sites where you can request information online. This is a significant benefit of the information age we now live in. The Internet provides access to as much information as one has the time to digest. In the so-called old days, you would call a franchisor, speak to the sales representative, and after providing some personal information, await franchise literature to arrive in the mail. Now you can obtain information from almost any franchisor without ever leaving the comfort of your home. Another advantage is that as you search a franchisor Web site, you may be able to identify their locations. This will indicate if the territory you desire is available.

4. Review the information you've requested to see if it meets the criteria of your interest, experience, and capital. Once you've narrowed your choices, you will want to speak to a franchisor salesperson in order to ask some key questions. With e-mail, you can even direct questions to the salesperson.

Information to gather from the franchisor:

- Is your territory available? How are territories defined? Are they exclusive?
- What is the investment range for the franchise?
- How would you describe the franchise process?
- What are the steps that are followed?
- What is the initial franchise fee? What do you receive?
- What is the ongoing royalty?
- Any other fees, such as for advertising fund?

- Briefly describe the support you will receive preopening and postopening.
- How many franchise locations have been added to the system in the past year? Any corporate-owned locations, and if yes, how many?

I would say that this discussion should take approximately thirty minutes to one hour. You should be able to gain a good overview of the franchise program. If the information you receive meets your expectations or goals, I would consider this a good franchise candidate for you. You may then begin to utilize a checklist or spreadsheet where you can enter key information for the franchise companies you are reviewing. This can be very useful in making comparisons, and ultimately, deciding upon the franchise company you wish to pursue.

Here is a sample of how you can set up a comparison chart of franchise opportunities. The information can be gathered from the Web site, response packet, UFOC, and interviews with the franchise salesperson.

Sample Franchise Comparison Checklist

Franchisors	A	B	C
Franchise since	1995	1992	2001
Franchise Fee	$15k	$13k	$20k
Ongoing Royalty	5%/sales	4%/sales	6%/sales
Franchise Term	5 years	5 years	10 years
Renewal Options	2-5 years	1-5 years	0
Territory (population)	50,000-75,000	40,000-60,000	100,000
Advertising Fund	N/A	1%/sales	N/A
Locations	150	250	60
Grand Opening Support	No	$1,000 in advert.	$2,500
Matching funds			
Training	3 days	3 days	5 days
Investment	$50-75k	$49-69k	$45-55k

You can use this format to develop your own checklist and add any other items you like. As an example, what do you receive for your franchise fee? Do you receive any software from the franchisor? Just because a royalty is higher, do you get "more for your money"?

Keep in mind that this checklist is a tool. You'll still need to follow through on all of the other steps necessary to make the right choice. You can use a tool like this to compare at a glance, however, you'll need to probe much deeper to have all of the important facts.

Now, let's return to the initial process. Once you have identified specific franchisors, you'll need to make contact with their headquarters. What you need to do is to identify territories that are available and request the initial franchise literature. Each franchisor has what is typically called a response packet, which consists of marketing material and literature that they send out to prospective franchisees. The response packet will present the franchise. It is primarily a marketing package that is intended to provide general information about the franchise and to encourage a candidate to take the next step. Franchisors provide this information to prospective franchisees because they want to give an overview of how the program works and answer initial questions that people typically ask. Today this information can usually be requested on the franchise Web-site.

After you've reviewed the response packet, you will most likely have a number of important questions. As I indicated previously, there are certain basic questions you'll want to ask. You should contact the franchise salesperson to get some of these questions answered. Be advised that some salespeople may be reluctant to get into a lot of detail until you submit an initial application and make a personal visit. From the salesperson's perspective, their intent is to move the candidate along in the sales process, but with the need to qualify the candidate. On your behalf, you want to be deliberate and disciplined in terms of following a specific plan or timetable. Obviously, visiting the franchisor headquarters takes time and expense. In most cases, the franchisor will expect the franchisee to pay for the visit, which is a further way of qualifying candidates. Some may refund the costs of the visit if you eventually acquire the franchise.

If you can get the salesperson to supply you with the names of certain franchisees, I would suggest you contact those franchisees before you make the visit to the franchisor corporate headquarters. Now, this may be somewhat of a reversal of what normally happens. However, I think it will give you insight and provide questions to ask before you go to the next step in the process. Some salespeople may be reluctant to provide you that information. They may tell you that the franchising process follows a certain protocol. Keep in mind, there is no law that says they have to follow a specific process, other than making sure that prior to or during the first face-to-face meeting they provide you with the Uniform Franchise Offering Circular or UFOC.

The UFOC contains franchisor information, the franchise agreement, and must meet requirements of the Federal Trade Commission. If you visit a franchisor at their headquarters, they are required to disclose or provide the UFOC to you at that time. Some may prefer to disclose you during your personal visit; however, there is no rule that says they can't mail you the UFOC. A good suggestion is when you speak to the salesperson, tell them how busy you are and that you can't take time out of your busy schedule to go and visit their headquarters without first seeing their franchise document. If you prevail upon the salesperson, they will likely provide you with the UFOC, especially if it means that they could lose a potential candidate. Most franchise salespeople receive a base salary and a commission or percentage of each franchise fee they bring in. Therefore, it is in their interest to process as many transactions as possible.

As a fallback position, you can usually access franchise locations on the franchisor's Web site and use this information to make initial calls to franchisees. However, be advised that many franchisees will be reluctant to give you any information until they check with their franchisor.

Once you receive the UFOC, you'll have a list of all of the current franchisees as well as those terminated within the last year. The major benefit is that you can select any franchisee you wish and contact them. Some salespeople give prospective franchisees, the names of certain franchisees that are called "validators." These are the franchisees that are fairly successful, have a good relationship with the franchisor, and generally have nothing bad to say about the program or the franchisor. That's why it is useful to call as many franchisees as possible and not just the ones you're provided.

Robert Kushell, president of Kushell Associates Inc. and a former director of the International Franchise Association, points out that a franchisor never really knows what kind of franchisee it is getting and the franchisee doesn't truly know what kind of franchisor he or she is getting.

Kushell suggests that prospective franchisees should request that they spend a day or two at a franchise unit so that the candidate can experience the reality of a franchise operation.

Kushell emphasizes the importance of prospective franchisees spending as much time with existing franchisees as possible. This could be done during personal visits or on the telephone. A key question to ask: "Is the franchisor there to help?"

Kushell makes the point that at the beginning of a franchise operation the franchisor typically understands everything about the business. As the system grows, the franchisor founders may become less involved and less aware of what takes place in the day-to-day operation of their franchisees.

A prospective franchisee needs to be sure that the franchisor listens to concerns. Kushell says, "You need to be sure the franchisor will be there for you in June as he was in January."

Following is a list of questions that I would suggest you ask the franchisees that you contact:

1. How long have you had the franchise?
2. How did you come to obtain the franchise? Were you referred by another franchisee? Was it through an advertisement?
3. Has the franchisor fulfilled the requirements that they said they would when you first met them? In other words, has the franchisor basically done what they promised?

4. Depending on the number of years that the franchisee has owned this business, ask if they have seen the franchisor make appropriate changes or enhancements to the franchise program over time. Some franchisors may do little to enhance the franchisee program, but rather, look for more franchisees to sign on without reinvesting into the franchise system.

5. Has the franchisee had any disputes or issues with the franchisor, and if so, how were they resolved? Who resolved the dispute? This is important, although most franchisees have had some problems, whether minor or major; certain franchisees are reluctant to bring a problem to the appropriate level. Many franchisors have field support to offer assistance at the local level and you want to be sure that the people who are in those positions are not only willing but also capable of helping you to resolve issues. As part of this question, you ought to find out what the persona or corporate culture is at the executive level of the franchisor. Obviously, this is going to depend on the size of the franchise. Although franchise companies are either large, middle size, or in a start-up mode, it is important to grasp a sense from the franchisees as to how they see the leadership of the franchise. Obviously, when you are dealing with the McDonalds of the world and other large systems, it becomes a whole different matter. However, most franchise systems are not the size of McDonalds.

6. Has the franchisee met his or her financial expectations? This is one of the most important questions you will ask since most franchisees are not going to be willing to tell you how much money they are making. By asking the question, "Have you reached your financial expectations or goals?" you will usually obtain the right response. This type of question may appear to be "closed end"; however; you will usually receive more than a yes or no response from the franchisee. Try to find out how long it took them to recover their investment and earn a profit.

7. Ask the franchisee if they had to do it over again would they still purchase the franchise. Don't be reluctant to open up on this subject.

Be sure that you speak to a large enough group of franchisees so that you have accurate feedback. I can't tell you how many prospective franchisees I have met who have called only one or two franchisees, and based upon those conversations, made a decision. Unfortunately, some of these decisions had negative outcomes; however, had some spoken to a larger group of franchisees they might have made a different decision, which in their case would have been the right one. Another point is that prospective franchisees will often call franchisees in their own geographic area. If a prospective franchisee is in the northeast, they will typically call franchisees in the northeast; if a franchisee is from the south, they may only call franchisees in the south, etc. I think it is important for prospective franchisees to call franchisees in different parts of the country as well as in the geographic area they are interested in. Also, a personal visit to franchisees is quite useful. Although many franchisees might be unwilling to spend the time, it's worth a try.

Craig Tractenberg, a well-known franchise attorney with Nixon Peabody, LLP, had a case many years ago where a franchisor used "validators" who were not franchisees but actually actors. Tractenberg filed an action against the franchisor for fraud and the FTC enjoined the franchisor from selling any more franchises. His recommendation is that prospective franchisees exercise caution when "validating" a franchise program and that they speak to as many franchisees as possible.

When a franchise program is successful, then the franchisees will be extolling the virtues of the franchise. This is a very important issue and you need to be a good listener to hear what these franchisees are saying. You need to read between the lines and listen very carefully as to what their experience has been and ask open-ended questions and follow up. If you ask them if they have met their financial expectations and they say yes, you want to ask if their goals have been exceeded. Try to develop a comfort level with the franchisees you speak to or visit and gather as much information from them as possible.

There is no doubt that the most important source of intelligence for a prospective franchisee will be gained from existing franchisees. Keep in mind, if you ask the sales person if they would suggest anyone that you should speak to, I can assure you they will give you franchisees that are good validators, we would refer to them as "singers." By this, I don't mean they will sing your favorite tune! You may also be told that if you call certain franchisees they may have had some issues in the past and could be somewhat negative. Don't be turned off by that because quite frankly, I have done that myself. I can recall several companies that I worked with where we had franchisees that were problematic, and not a result of anything we did or didn't do as a franchisor. So don't be discouraged by that comment. In fact, that kind of candor can be refreshing and helpful.

I present this process as the first step in evaluating the franchise that you have chosen. In many cases, you will find this process will be recommended at the very end of the cycle or at the point when one is ready to acquire the franchise. My experience has been that when prospective franchisees interview existing franchisees, at the very end of the franchising process, they may be less prone to consider what the franchisees say. Once a prospective franchisee has gone through most of the franchising processes to include reviewing the UFOC, meeting the franchisor at their headquarters, and getting most of their questions answered, then they are almost ready to acknowledge that this is the franchise for them. Therefore, when they interview existing franchisees, they are already close to making a positive decision.

I strongly recommend that the process of interviewing franchisees takes place at the beginning rather than at the end of the process with follow-up where necessary. You will be much more objective and open-minded at that time. Moreover, these discussions can generate questions you will want to ask the franchisor. One thing that you need to be cognizant of when speaking to existing franchisees is that it is human nature that no one likes to admit failure or to acknowledge that they have made the wrong decision. Be aware of this fact when you speak to existing franchisees. Even those who might not have been as successful as they would have hoped may still recommend the franchise.

I have seen cases where franchisees who have not done well financially become excellent validators, primarily because they were unwilling to acknowledge to a prospective franchisee that things have not worked out as well as they would have liked. Therefore, they will react in a very positive way to the franchise candidate even though they might have had problems. The most effective way of evaluating the franchise program and the franchisor begins with you speaking to existing franchisees and asking the right questions. Once again, to highlight the key questions or information that you want to elicit from the existing franchisees:

> Did they reach or exceed their financial expectations regarding this franchise?

> Were the services and/or benefits that the franchisor promised when the franchisee first bought the franchise delivered?

> If they encountered any issues with the franchisor, was there a process for resolving these issues or disputes? How does the franchisor handle dispute resolution?

> What was the background of the franchisee before they bought the franchise? If you ask the franchisees this question, then you will develop a sense as to what strengths and attributes the existing franchisees brought to this franchise when they first began. You may find a common thread among the franchisees you speak to. In point of fact, if you are evaluating more than one franchise, but with certain similarities, these kinds of questions will lead to a list of attributes that these

people share. Of course, the key issue is, how do you compare to them in terms of your own background, experience, skills, etc.

This last question is without a doubt the most important to ask each franchisee. What do they think are the most significant ingredients for success in this particular franchise? Let them tell you what they think is most important in order to be successful. You will learn a lot that way. I also think that even those who have not done as well as they would have liked will tell you what they think are the critical success factors. Asking these kinds of questions will give you a good indication from existing franchisees what they think makes for success in this franchise.

I have devoted a good deal of time on the subject of interviewing existing franchisees. As I explained at the outset, this may run counter to what you may find in certain franchise books or hear from franchise attorneys or advisors. Usually, you will follow certain steps and the last one is interviewing franchisees. As I've said before, you need to do this at the very beginning of your franchise evaluation process.

This first step is important even from a franchisor standpoint. As an example, during my career, I have evaluated prospective business or franchise opportunities as acquisition targets. One of the first things that I would do in evaluating a potential franchise company was to speak with as many franchisees as I could. This gave me the opportunity to determine from the franchisees how they evaluated this particular franchise company. If I worked in reverse and I looked at the franchise concept first with an eye toward introducing it in my company, then I might not have gotten a true sense as to how successful that concept was.

I can recall one company I was evaluating. I obtained the UFOC and called a number of franchisees. Most were quite candid and did not have the most positive comments about the franchise. That is a true red flag because if franchisees are going to be that outspoken to a prospective franchisee then they must be really having problems. However, their concern was not getting the service they needed, but rather, they did not achieve the financial return that they had anticipated when they bought the franchise. The franchisees I spoke to told me, if you did not have a minimum amount of revenue than you were going to be in a difficult position to earn any kind of profit. The pro forma revenue levels were not realistic. In fact, they were what I would consider to be at a minimum threshold. Based upon my analysis, I determined that we should not acquire this company.

I obviously knew the questions to ask, and quite frankly, they're the same questions I just presented to you in this chapter. It is very easy to put things down on paper, to set financial models in place; however, it is another thing to find out what happens in the real world. This is why I think franchising provides you a significant advantage that you will not find in other industries. You can speak to people that are already doing what you are looking to do. You have the opportunity to find out from them how successful one can be and what it takes to be successful.

Here is another way to evaluate a franchise program.

Identify what it would cost for the services that the franchisor is providing. If you think you could do it for less cost, good luck to you and perhaps the best approach is to do it yourself. I think that is something that most prospective franchisees do not consider as part of the decision-making process. Namely, pricing and evaluating the services that they are going to receive. If one gets involved in a highly recognized franchise, with significant name recognition, and a proven track record of success, that's an entirely different matter. However, out of the numerous franchise programs that are available in the United States, most do not have strong name recognition like the larger franchisors.

Therefore, it's reasonable for you to price the services that you are going to receive from the franchisor and to make sure that the services are worth the fees that you are paying, whether it is in the form of an ongoing royalty and/or the initial franchise fee.

Another fact to consider when evaluating the value of the brand or the marks is the significance of the name. By this, consider the example of a franchisor that may have 100 locations in the eastern part of the United States. You are a prospective franchisee who will forge new ground in the western United States. Since, the franchise you are joining has limited brand recognition and is not a large franchisor, its name may not be well known outside of its current operating area. What this means is that you are going to be a pioneer. You should never forget this fact when you are considering a franchise, particularly a new one, since you will be the one who is going to deliver the message. Keep this in mind if you desire to buy the franchise. You may request some concessions from the franchisor for advertising, marketing, etc.

All of this information gathering should give you a significant benefit in evaluating the franchise that you are considering. Before you get too far involved in the process and into a situation when you start spending money for advisors, attorneys, and accountants, you will already have a comfort level, and hopefully, a positive feeling about the particular franchise that you are interested in.

When you enter the next step in the process, which is to review the franchise agreement and meet the franchisor, you will have already done a good amount of background work. You've already gained an understanding pertaining to the track record and the performance of the franchisor by speaking with its franchisees.

Let's recap what you have been able to accomplish at this point:

1. You have gained a significant insight into particular franchisors and the franchise companies that you are evaluating, and you have been able to do it on your own.
2. You haven't had to go out and spend significant money to have someone read the UFOC.

3. You haven't had an accountant perform an elaborate cash flow analysis.

The bottom line is, before you take that next step which involves starting to spend some of your financial capital, you have already been able to gain a good amount of information. This is important, since most prospective franchisees do not have a stream of working capital where they can hire advisors to evaluate prospective franchisors.

In summary, the key step after you have selected the franchise companies that interest you are to gain as much information about that franchise as possible. I can assure you, after spending more than twenty-five years in franchising, those prospective franchisees that rely on someone else to do their bidding will usually find themselves disappointed after the fact.

Now that you have had an opportunity to select or gain additional information pertaining to the franchise programs that you want to pursue, the next step is to review the UFOC in detail. Some franchisors may be reluctant to send you the UFOC through the mail. This basically means that you may have to visit the franchisor on sight in order to get a UFOC. However, this does not mean that you can't request one. Over the years, my practice has been to forward an individual a copy of the UFOC if they requested it prior to visiting our corporate offices. Companies such as *www.franchisehelp.com* can provide a UFOC for a slight fee. Once you have received the UFOC, it is important to review all of the different sections within that document, and most important, knowing what to look for.

The next chapter deals with evaluating the franchisor. This is where you start to get into the details of how the franchisor operates, what their franchise agreement is like, and what are the financial risks and rewards that lie ahead.

CHAPTER 3

Evaluating the Franchise

*It's easier for a franchisor to recover from
choosing the wrong franchisee than vice versa.*

By now, you should have interviewed a number of
franchisees from one or more franchise companies. If you've been
comfortable with the answers that you've received from the
franchisees, then your next step is to review the UFOC and plan
to meet with the franchisor.

Although anyone can obtain and read a UFOC, I strongly
advise those who are interested in obtaining a franchise to utilize
a competent franchise attorney to review the UFOC and offer
advice before making a final decision and signing any franchise
documents. At the outset, you may wish to conduct a preliminary
review yourself if you have the requisite business experience.

Some franchisors have a policy that the UFOC will be
provided to a prospective franchisee during the candidate's visit
to the franchisor's corporate headquarters. Many franchisors feel
that if the prospective franchisee receives the UFOC before a

meeting and has certain objections, the candidate may decide that they do not want to visit with the franchisor until certain items have been negotiated. Also, most franchisors will not engage in negotiating terms of the franchise agreement until they have met the prospective franchisee in person. That was my position as well. Upon request, I would forward a copy of the UFOC to a candidate; however, I would not negotiate any changes to the franchise agreement until I met them.

There were a number of instances where I would assign one of my field staff to meet a prospective franchisee. This provided me an excellent opportunity to have one of my subordinates who was familiar with the franchise territory and experienced in marketing and operations to meet the candidate face-to-face and give me their feedback.

As a prospective franchisee, you may find it useful to meet with the regional or district manager before going to visit corporate headquarters. You should try to arrange a meeting with this type of individual since you'll gain insight from someone who works directly with the franchisees. At this level in the franchisor organization, you should be better able to gather information regarding marketing and sales programs, training, available resources, and ongoing support. The field people are usually those closest to the franchisees and as such very knowledgeable regarding the franchise operation. If you don't have an opportunity to meet the field representative first, be sure that you do have the opportunity to at least speak with them before you make your final decision.

My objective over the years has been to have prospective franchisees visit our corporate franchise headquarters first. In this way, we could provide an informative presentation and present our story to the franchisee. Of course, if a franchisee wanted to review the UFOC prior to the visit, then we would send them a copy of the document. It is anticipated that at some time in the future, franchisors will be able to deliver their UFOC "online" to prospective franchisees. Eventually the UFOC will be e-mailed to candidates and their attorneys. The regulatory authorities are working out the details of this practice. There are Web sites, which will e-mail UFOCs upon request for a slight fee.

The Uniform Franchise Offering Circular is a document that is governed under the guidelines of the Federal Trade Commission and supplemented by regulatory requirements on the part of several states. In the appendix, you will find a list of the states that require some form of filing or registration of the UFOC. If you reside in one of these states or the franchisor operates and seeks franchisees from a registration state, you or your attorney should confirm that the UFOC is filed or compliant in that state.

The UFOC contains a framework of twenty-three questions or categories of information to which the franchisor must respond. This information gives a prospective franchisee a good deal of knowledge pertaining to the franchisor, ranging from the background and history of the company, its executives and key officers, to the financial performance and condition of the franchisor. I suggest you review the UFOC using the information that I presented below. You should always engage a franchise attorney to read the document. Even though you will utilize the services of an attorney, you can read the UFOC yourself to gain information. There are certain items that are contained in the UFOC that you will want to focus on. In this chapter, I'll tell you what these items are, why they are important, and what you should look for.

When you first discuss the UFOC and the franchise agreement with the franchise salesperson, it is important to ask if any of the terms are negotiable. It is safe to say that, in certain cases, a mature or highly developed franchisor may be reluctant to negotiate many terms of the franchise agreement. Typically, the more eager the franchisor is to bring on new franchisees and expand their network, the more willing they may be to negotiate the agreement. If I had several prospective franchisees interested in a particular market or territory, I would be in a position to be much more demanding and less willing to negotiate away certain terms of the agreement. The concept is the same for all business transactions. Who has the edge, the buyer or the seller? Be aware of this fact at all times and don't dismiss a franchisor simply because they are unwilling to negotiate the agreement. After all, most people would welcome owning a McDonalds franchise with the franchise agreement fully intact. You simply need to be cautious when dealing with certain provisions of the franchise agreement. You should not take anything for granted and view those provisions in the franchise agreement that you and your attorney are concerned with by asking questions of the franchisor.

Many franchisors will have certain items in the franchise agreement that they are more willing to negotiate than others. Conversely, there are certain items within a franchise agreement I would call "non-negotiable items." These are the sections that are almost never changed.

These "non-negotiable items" would include, but may not be limited to, the length or term of the agreement, the initial franchise fee (although some franchisors may finance part of the fee), royalty payments, no exclusivity of the territory, and the termination provisions.

As indicated previously, the Uniform Franchise Offering Circular contains twenty-three key items. The UFOC also includes the actual franchise agreement itself. Some of the more important items to review are detailed below. My suggestion is to read these sections more than once, and unless you are highly skilled in franchising, be sure your attorney reviews the UFOC as well.

Mario Herman, an attorney based in Washington DC, who has represented numerous franchisees explains what he considers important when reviewing the UFOC and the franchisor:

> "I focus on the amount of experience a franchisor has in terms of years, the franchisee turnover rate, whether the franchisor is a "professional" franchisor and knows a good deal about the business being franchised. Is the franchisor undercapitalized and does the franchisor rely more on up-front fees

versus ongoing royalties? I also look to what can be learned from former franchisees. What is the litigation history of the franchisor, especially with respect to fraud and misrepresentation, the previous business experience of the principals and whether any earnings claims are provided in the UFOC or more subtly through oral statements? I look at the termination, closure and resale information in the UFOC as well as financial statements of the franchisor and any previous bankruptcies related to the principals. Other areas include how onerous the termination and expiration provisions are, as well as buybacks and rights of first refusal. Lastly, the working capital requirements for a franchisee should be realistic. Finally, can my client really obtain equity in the business over time." Although you'll read the UFOC yourself, be sure you have competent franchise counsel to review it.

Following is an overview of the sections in the UFOC document:

Item 1   "The Franchisor—its Predecessors and Affiliates."— This section gives a history of the franchise, to include its origination and if there were any major acquisitions or major changes regarding the franchisor. This is the information that gives you the background of the franchisor. Also, how long the franchisor has been franchising and certain competitive factors. It is in this section that you'll learn about how the franchise was started. You'll find the opportunity to perhaps identify some questions you might have thought of prior to reading item 1.

Item 2   "Business Experience"—Depicts the business experience of the franchisor and its key officers. This will give you a profile of the franchisor and the people who are operating the franchise. The business experience section, which is item 2 of the UFOC, has to show at least a minimum of five year's history for each of the key officers or executives who are employed by the franchisor. Pay careful attention to this section because it will give you the background of these individuals. You want to be sure these short resumes reflect the proper level of experience and understanding regarding the franchise that you are looking to acquire.

Item 3   "Litigation"—This section will list all of the litigation that the franchisor has been involved with, both past and present. The period covered is typically ten years. Although there are rules regarding how "material" the litigation is, all litigation will be included in this section. By the way, if the litigation has ended, the nature of how it ended must be disclosed. This would include settlements or judgments. Be careful, however, since not all the litigation may be averse to the franchisor. Franchisor litigation is not necessarily bad; however, it requires a trained eye to determine the distinction. Litigation is an area, where unless you have some legal expertise or background, you need to rely on your attorney for insight.

Item 4   "Bankruptcy"—If anyone listed in items 1 and 2 of the UFOC has been involved as a debtor under the Federal Bankruptcy Code, Title 11 it will be disclosed here.

Item 5   "Initial Franchise Fee"—This section will set forth the initial franchise fee paid and the circumstances under which the fee may be refunded or reduced.

Item 6   "Other Fees"—This section shows a table, which lists all of the fees the franchisee pays. It shows the name of the fee, amount of the fee, due date, and remarks. This information is presented in an easy-to-read format. Be sure you fully understand each of your financial obligations as presented in this section.

Item 7   "Initial Investment"—presents a range of the investment that one would make in the franchise, including the initial franchise fee, estimated cost of a lease, equipment, grand opening expense, and working capital for three months. Typically, the initial investment section includes three months of operating costs. You will see a range, which includes the working capital and all the other expenses that will be incurred by the franchisee. This is the section where you will have an opportunity to gain an understanding as to what your investment will be for the franchise business. My practice as a franchise executive was to be conservative in this section. I wanted to have an investment range that may be a little high rather than too low. The last thing I wanted was to have a new franchisee finding out after several months of operations that their investment was going to be higher than what they anticipated.

Since the investment numbers do not convert to a break-even point, some franchisees will find that they have exceeded the investment number in this table, not recognizing that the table presents short-term investment requirements. Your experience in this area will provide substance for further discussions with franchisees of that system and questions for the franchisor.

Item 8   "Restrictions on Sources of Products and Services"— This section describes rights in acquiring certain products, services, supplies, or equipment that might be required to be purchased from the franchisor. You will need to understand exactly what you can or cannot purchase without franchisor's approval. In some cases, they may be required to purchase products from only the franchisor. Some franchisors have strict controls on certain purchases in order to protect the franchise standards and its trade name. Most food franchises will have strict requirements regarding this area, and rightfully so. Be sure you fully understand what the rules are when it comes to purchasing supplies and services

Item 9   "Franchisee's Obligations"—sets forth all of the obligations of the franchisee in a very straightforward format that defines your obligations and where those appear in the franchise agreement by specific section. The obligations are also referenced in the UFOC section where they appear. This will give a simple overview of what your responsibilities, as a franchisee will be. This section reflects one of the more beneficial changes that was made to the UFOC in recent years, since it gives prospective franchisees an easy way of identifying what all of their obligations are.

Item 10   "Financing"—provides information on financing that may be provided by the franchisor. A few franchisors provide direct financial assistance to qualifying franchisees, although this is rare. Many will direct candidates to third party financing, such as the SBA, etc. In most cases, the comment will be that "the franchisor offers no financing to its franchisees."

Item 11   "Franchisor Obligations"—describes the franchisor obligations in providing products, services, equipment, and support to the franchisees. There are schedules on training, the composition of the training, and where it is held. A table of contents from the operations manual will be included as an exhibit in the UFOC. By the way, since the franchise operations manual is referenced in virtually all franchise agreements, some franchise attorneys will request a loan of the operations manual so they can review it with their client. Franchise agreements are carefully written so that changes in policies and procedures can be made via the operations manual. Some language states these changes cannot materially alter the financial obligation of the franchisee. This prevents the franchisor from making changes to the franchise agreement under the pretext of a change in the operations manual, which can result in the franchisee paying more fees or incurring additional costs.

Item 12 "Territory"—defines the territory and the rights a franchisee has regarding the territory and whether the franchisee has exclusivity regarding the territory, which prevents another location from being opened. In some cases a franchisor will allow sales being made into another franchisee territory. Be sure that you thoroughly understand your rights regarding your territory. Certain franchisors will prevent their franchisees from conducting business outside of the franchisee's territory. Can the franchisor operate under a different brand name in your territory? Can other franchisees sell into your territory? Is this a bad thing?

Item 13 "Trademarks"—In this section you'll find the franchisor trademarks and any registrations with the United States Patent Office. This is very important since it represents the brands and identities you'll be marketing.

Item 14 "Patents, Copyrights, and Proprietary Information"—This section will detail any patents or copyrights held by the franchisor. The items usually included in this section will be the manuals, advertising, marketing literature, and promotional materials. Also language pertaining to confidential and proprietary information will be set forth in this section.

Item 15 "Obligation to Participate in the Operation of the Franchise"—In this section some provisions require that the franchisee devote full-time to the franchise while other provisions may allow a manager to operate in place of the franchisee, providing the manager is "qualified" and/or approved by the franchisor.

Item 16 "Restrictions on What the Franchisee May Sell"—shows any restrictions on what can or cannot be sold from the franchise location by the franchisee.

Item 17 "Renewal, Termination, Transfer, and Dispute Resolution"—Presented in a table, this section shows the provision, location in the franchise agreement, and a summary regarding the term of your agreement, the process to follow in the event you wish to sell or assign your franchise agreement, termination provisions, and how disputes may be resolved. This section is important since the franchisee may very well desire to sell the business in the future. In almost every single franchise agreement, the franchisor has the right of first refusal, which means if a franchisee wishes to sell the franchise, the franchisor has the option of acquiring the franchise, upon the same terms and conditions offered by a prospective buyer. There are many other important provisions contained within this section. This section also contains the termination provision whereby the franchisor can default and/or terminate the franchisee. Be sure to review this section and the table, which details each default and termination provision.

Item 18 Public Figures—This section will list any public figures or celebrities who endorse or promote the franchise.

Item 19 "Earnings Claims"—If the franchisor presents an earnings claim, which shows the history of revenue or financial results achieved by the franchisees, it will be disclosed and presented in this section. By the way, if a franchisor does not report an earnings claim under item 19 then they are obliged to refrain from representing franchisee sales or earnings to prospective franchisees. This is a method for an unethical franchisor to conveniently avoid any questions about franchisee results, which could confuse a prospect.

Item 20 "List of Outlets"—One of the most important sections in the UFOC. This section contains the following three charts or schedules:

Chart 1 lists all of the franchise locations for a three-year period by state and will show, over the course of the three-year period, franchise terminations, if the franchisor had acquired

any franchises or if any franchisees had left
the system. This will show changes and
causal factors regarding number of franchise
locations. You will be able to see trends and
changes in the number of franchisees. What
you want to do is to look, not only by state
but, most important, at the totals on the
bottom of the table of chart 1. Look at the
terminations and also the growth in the
number of franchises over this three-year
period. When the franchisor has bought
back a franchise, it will also be shown in
this chart. You'll know how many franchisees
were acquired by the franchisor, sold to other
franchisees, terminated, expired, or left the
system outright. The totals in the last
column show the number of franchise
locations in operation at the end of each year.
Chart 2 shows the status of corporately owned
centers over a three-year period. When you
look at this table, you will get an indication
of activity in terms of corporate store growth.
It will show you what kind of emphasis the
franchisor places on growing corporate
offices. As an example, let's assume that in
chart 1 you find that the growth of franchise
locations has been declining versus two or
three years ago, and on chart 2, you see the
growth of corporately owned offices has been
increasing versus two or three years ago. This
may indicate that the franchisor is shifting
emphasis from a network of franchises to
corporate operations. On the other hand, it
may show that the franchisor is attempting
to achieve a balance of franchise and corporate

locations, which quite frankly, might be an advantage to the franchisor and the network from a financial standpoint. In some cases, a balance between franchise and corporate locations, be they retail, etc., might be advantageous to the franchisor versus a network of purely franchise locations. Don't draw the conclusion that simply because corporate locations are growing as opposed to franchise locations that this is necessarily a negative occurrence. The important point is to look at the "numbers" and question certain trends that you see.

Chart 3 The franchisor is required to show what their projected growth in new locations is for the next year by state. This chart is rarely reliable since it merely reflects the franchisor's business plan.

Item 21 "Financial Statements"—contains the financial statements of the franchisor. This will tell you about the franchisor from a financial standpoint and gives you a snapshot of their financial health. If it's a fairly new franchisor, there will be less financial information and history than a franchisor that is more mature. This means that you will have less information upon which to base an independent financial evaluation. On the other hand, if you are dealing with a more mature franchisor, which may be a publicly held company, there will be a wealth of information not only contained in the UFOC, but also available through their public financial reports that they are required to file by statute. Franchisors are required to have financial statements that are current or no more than one hundred twenty days old from their financial anniversary.

Item 22 "Contracts"—This section will refer to the contracts you are required to sign as a franchisee. The franchise agreement, which is included with the UFOC, will be referenced.

Item 23 "Receipt"—This section identifies the receipt, which is to be signed by the prospective franchisee at least ten (10) business days before the franchise agreement is signed.

"The Franchise Agreement"—Regulators made a number of changes to the UFOC several years ago, which among other things required that the information in the UFOC be presented in easily, understood language. Also, that particular information is presented in tables and schedules. The UFOC can be described as "explaining" the franchise agreement in general terms. However, the actual franchise agreement is a complex contract, which represents the business agreement you will operate under. It's the document you will sign and be expected to abide by. In chapter 5, I present the key areas of the franchise agreement and suggest those provisions, which could be negotiated.

Since franchise agreements will vary from company to company, I will refrain from describing each section. However, all of the agreements will contain certain common provisions.

Ignacio Morrell, an executive who had worked for a prominent franchisor, was in the process of buying his own franchise. As part of this process Mr. Morrell developed a list of the four most important attributes he looked for in a franchisor.

These items were as follows:

1. A clearly articulated and unique system or concept. The franchisor must be able to logically tell you what is special about the business concept. Listen carefully when evaluating this point.

2. Consistent system standards throughout the franchise network. You need to look at how much the franchisor

invests in manuals, training, and maintaining standards throughout the network. Ask the franchisees if they embrace the system and its standards.

3. The franchisor must generate a sincere passion for the success of its franchisees. Is the franchisor more concerned with selling new franchisees and territories in order to earn initial fees? Is the franchisor concerned with building a national network in order to sell the company to the investment community?

4. The franchisor with a proven track record will always be more attractive than one with less of a record to review. It doesn't mean that all franchisors must have years of experience but rather that they have enough of a track record to warrant your investment.

These items are useful to keep in mind as you evaluate your specific franchise opportunities.

CHAPTER 4

Meeting the Franchisor

Your only opportunity to meet the franchisor
face-to-face before making your decision.

By now, you have had an opportunity to interview a number of franchisees and should, hopefully, have received answers to the questions that you asked. You and your attorney should have reviewed the UFOC and the franchise agreement either in detail or preliminarily. Whatever sequence of events you have followed, a critical part of this process is to meet with the franchisor at corporate headquarters.

You'll meet the individuals who will be responsible for providing you the services that you are obligated to receive. Whether it is a "discovery day" or another term that the franchisor uses, most franchisors will have the prospective franchisees visit their corporate headquarters. The reason is obvious: This is an important decision for the franchisee as well as for the franchisor, and by having the prospective franchisee visit their corporate headquarters, the franchisee will have an opportunity to learn about the franchisor programs and meet key personnel on a face-to-face basis. It also gives the franchisors' staff the opportunity to meet the candidate and review their qualifications.

Franchisors use various methods for presenting their program and screening franchise candidates. In some cases, a few select individuals will meet the franchisee and they will have the responsibility for screening and approving each franchise candidate. In other cases, five or six franchisor staff members, including the president or CEO, may meet the prospective franchisee. My preference was to use the corporate visit as an opportunity to meet the franchisee and to have the franchisee meet the important members of the franchise team. Whatever the objectives of the franchisor, chances are that you will be going into the corporate headquarters with an opportunity to meet their key representatives. Part of the agenda will include a franchisor presentation usually made by the salesperson with support from his colleagues.

Harold Kestenbaum, a New York attorney with Farrell Fritz, who has represented numerous franchisors and franchisees over the course of twenty-five years, offers some insight into this process: "There are many aspects to the evaluation of a franchisor by a prospective franchisee not the least of which is the professionalism and way that the franchisor handles the first face-to-face meeting with the franchise prospect at franchisor headquarters. Franchisees are very astute and they can easily detect whether a franchisor handles the personal meeting in a professional manner or in a nonchalant way, which can convey a message of indifference to the prospect that it doesn't matter whether or not the franchisee buys the franchise. Whoever is representing the franchisor, they need to be attentive to the franchise candidate and answer all of their questions no matter how insignificant they may appear. The salesperson should not make earnings claims when none are disclosed under item 19 of the UFOC. Furthermore, the prospective franchisee should feel that they are wanted and that their time spent is appreciated. The conduct and professionalism of the entire franchisor staff will send a message to the prospect as to whether this is the company he or she would want to be associated with."

As to the above, I suggest that you make a point to meet the president or CEO of the franchise company unless there is a very good reason this cannot be done. In fact, the franchise organizations that I have worked with had a requirement to inform the president and other key staff when a prospective franchisee would be visiting the corporate headquarters. This way, they would be available to meet the candidate. There are some franchisors who set aside a complete day for the meeting with a detailed agenda which gives the franchisee and the franchisor an opportunity to meet each other and a chance for the franchisor to present its company and its people. This is their chance to show the prospective franchisee that they have the tools and the capability to help the franchisee be successful.

From your perspective as a candidate, this is your opportunity to demonstrate to the franchisor that you have the wherewithal and the ability to be a successful franchisee. No franchisor, except those who quite frankly are not operating in an ethical manner, would want to sign up franchisees who have a high risk of failure. Once again, I have been fortunate to have worked for ethical franchisors my entire career and I know of no case where there was a franchisee brought on without us believing that they had a high probability for success. This is what we always wanted to do and this is what we felt was our objective. At the end of this chapter I listed a number of questions that you should ask the representatives of the franchisor. I have also listed some topics or subjects that should be discussed. This is an important part of the process because this is your chance to be able to have the opportunity to meet the franchisor and all of its key staff and evaluate their commitment to you and the franchise program.

My comment had always been, "This is akin to a courtship." It is an opportunity for both parties to get to know each other before they make that very important decision to "walk down the aisle," so to speak, and establish a relationship under the franchise agreement.

During the meeting, you should be able to raise some of the questions that pertain to the franchise agreement, particularly those items that you feel you would like to negotiate and this is the opportune time to bring those issues up. From a franchisor standpoint, I enjoyed the opportunity to meet with prospective franchisees face-to-face and have them bring up questions or issues. I would encourage you to take this same approach. When you are with the franchisor, it is the right time to discuss the key items in the franchise agreement.

David Savitsky, CEO of ATC Healthcare Services Inc., offers this advice, "Meeting the franchisor is the most important step you'll take in deciding whether or not a specific franchise is right for you. Before the meeting, do your homework and find out all you can about the franchisor. Prepare a list of questions relevant to the franchise business and be sure you get satisfactory answers. Don't just think 'start-up,' but ongoing support, training, and building a long-term relationship. If you leave the meeting with the same questions or new ones that were not answered to your satisfaction, walk away from the opportunity. If you like what you heard, then take the next step."

Since this is going to be a function of whether you had the UFOC before this meeting, you can understand why you should obtain it prior to your meeting. If you have had an opportunity to review the UFOC and you have some items that you would like to negotiate in the franchise agreement, I would suggest that during your meeting with the franchisor, stay with those more salient points and those items that are important.

I have met with prospective franchisees that raised two or three points that they felt were important, and would indicate that they may have other points, but that these are the critical ones. These were what, in the business world, we would refer to as the "deal breakers," namely those items that either party feels must be resolved or the deal is basically doomed. I think if you have a sense as to what some of these items are, a good time to bring them up would be during your meeting with the franchisor.

While you are meeting with the franchisor, take every opportunity to observe and gain an understanding as to the franchisor's "personality." You need to be very objective and yet at the same time obtain as much information as you can. I have had instances where prospective franchisees would not participate in the meeting alone, but rather, bring their spouse, a friend, or an advisor. This is a good idea. Depending upon the nature of the visit, it will give you an opportunity to have a second opinion. I do recall having had a woman visit me who was interested in a franchise. She brought her husband who happened to be a practicing psychologist and during all of our meetings, I felt like I was being psychoanalyzed. Every word that I was saying was under the watchful eyes of her husband. We had a good laugh about this after they left. By the way, we felt she was not qualified to buy the franchise. I would suggest, depending on the arrangements, to bring another person with you to observe and make a contribution to your decision. This is a major step in your career and you will be investing hard-earned monies in the franchise venture, so you want to be sure that you have done your homework and make the best decision for you. Be sure that the franchisor approves this visitor in advance.

Following is a list of questions that I would ask the franchisor during your visit. In fact, it might not be a bad idea before your visit to indicate to the franchisor or salesperson that you do have certain questions, several in particular that are important. You want to be sure that you meet with the individuals who can answer these questions. The more that you can be in control of the meeting from the standpoint of gaining information, the more productive your visit will be. Don't forget, you are the one investing the money and it's easier for a franchisor to recover from choosing the wrong franchisee than vice versa! Some advice: Don't provide all of the questions prior to your meeting. By "springing" certain questions on the franchisor during your personal visit, you may gain some additional insight based upon the franchisor's response.

You want to be sure that you'll meet the individuals who are most important to your franchise operation and to personally meet those individuals who in some way will be impacting your role as a franchisee. In addition to the questions you and your advisors will develop, here are some questions and topics that you should bring up and discuss during your visit.

1. Find out if the franchisor has a strategic plan and specific goals for the franchise system. Does the franchisor have a program or objective to open a certain amount of franchises to grow to a certain size, etc? I think that this is important and something you would want to find out about. What are the specific growth plans for the franchisor, for the short term as well as for the long term? Are there any geographic areas that the franchisor will be concentrating on?

2. Does the franchisor have national meetings or a convention? If they do, approximately what percent of the franchisees attend this meeting? This can give you some indication as to how well received the franchisor is by the franchisees. It is something that one might not necessarily consider, but if you are looking at a franchise program and they have a national meeting that is not well attended by the franchisees, then clearly, the franchisees may feel that they are not gaining very much by attending this particular event.

3. Are there quarterly meetings or regional meetings for the franchisees? Some franchisors that I have been with would have meetings in certain geographic areas once a year in addition to a national meeting. This would give the franchisees the opportunity to be able to hear about new programs and also to learn more about what objectives and goals the franchisor has.

4. Does the franchisor have a newsletter? What kind of information does the franchisor provide the franchisees in terms of communication?

5. I would ask the franchisor representative to see some sample reports that are provided to the franchisees. Are

there specific reports that are provided on a regular basis? Are there reports, which show the top performing franchisees in sales, etc.?

6. Does the franchisor have any sales contests or promotions for their franchisees? I have been involved with some franchisors where we would periodically run sales contests, which were intended to create a level of enthusiasm for the franchisees by having prizes and other rewards.

7. Does the franchise system have a Franchise Advisory Council? How long have they had a FAC? How are the franchisee members selected or chosen to participate on the FAC? How often does the FAC meet? Who does the franchise advisory council meet with from the franchisor?

8. What does the franchisor provide for its franchisees regarding health insurance and other benefits? Do they have a preferred vendor that franchisees can utilize?

9. How is the franchise organized from a technology standpoint? Is there system-wide e-mail? Inventory data line? How does it compare with competitors?

10. Who are the top franchisees in sales? You don't need the sales amount, but who they are.

You will obviously need to ask questions that are more specific to the franchise opportunity. Based upon the result of your interviewing franchisees, the review of the franchise agreement and UFOC as well as other sources of information, you'll be able to have specific questions unique to this particular franchisor and its organization.

My suggestion is to gain a sense as to the culture of the franchisor. You need to be careful to listen to the response after asking the franchisor questions. You need to take full advantage of this opportunity to gain a level of trust and confidence in the franchisor. Don't forget the agreement you will be ultimately signing will depend in good measure upon the performance of the franchisor, its staff, and the franchise program, which will afford you the opportunity for success. Do you feel, based upon all of the information you've gathered, that they will "deliver as promised"?

As I indicated earlier, I would urge you to have someone with some business experience accompany you on this visit unless it is not financially feasible. By having someone else involved, you will have the benefit of someone who may be more objective and are able to give you quality feedback.

This is your opportunity to have a preliminary discussion regarding the items in the franchise agreement that you would like to change or amend. The next chapter presents information on negotiating the franchise agreement. However, this process can follow several steps. In some cases, you may already know from your attorney what items you want to negotiate in which case you may present them during this meeting. The other method which I would recommend is that since you'll make a final decision regarding the franchise only after your visit, you should meet with your attorney to review and discuss requested changes to the franchise agreement at that point. I would suggest that this is the most effective way to proceed since you will base your final decision regarding the purchase of the franchise on the results of your personal visit. Therefore, you won't go through all the time and expense at this stage. Your attorney may very well recommend the process you should follow whether you negotiate during your visit, after your visit, whether your attorney negotiates on your behalf, etc.

From the franchisor's perspective, you must recognize that the franchisor staff is going to make a determination and decision as to whether they feel you are qualified to be one of their franchisees. Related to this fact is that many franchise companies go through a growth cycle which runs something like this: The franchisor that is just beginning will be a little more forgiving in terms of the qualifications of the franchisees. Although most won't admit it, when one is trying to grow as a franchisor, one wants to have as many new franchisees as possible. History is full of franchisors that unfortunately sold more franchisees than they could support. However, some franchisors would like to have that problem. Therefore, the ability of a franchisee to meet and fulfill the qualifications of the franchisor will depend in great measure upon the business maturity of the franchisor.

You should realize that a mature franchise network with fewer franchises available to sell is going to be much more selective than one that is in the early stages of growth. The franchisor wants to make sure that you are not only qualified financially, but also from an aptitude and experience standpoint. They want to make sure that you possess the tools for success.

I can assure you that franchisors do not sell franchises expecting franchisees to fail, but rather, they want franchisees to be successful. I have had the experience to work for many franchisors during my career and we never wanted to see a franchisee fail. That's something that we would try to avoid at all costs, although there were certain instances where it was unavoidable. As is the case with hiring an employee, not every decision is correct; however, an employee can be terminated much easier than a franchisee. This is another reason why franchisors want to select the right franchise candidate.

As you are going through your process during the visit, always keep in mind that the franchisor is evaluating you and wants to be sure that you are the right person. Hopefully, you have been able to have a positive visit with the franchisor and you have resolved the items that you wanted to, with the result that you will sign what you feel is a fair franchise agreement. Keep in mind, it is important that you utilize legal counsel to advise and assist you in this final step because once you sign that agreement, you put your name "on the line."

I might add that many franchisors will require a personal guarantee, which means that as a franchisee, you will personally guarantee the obligations of the franchise you acquire. What this means is that if the franchise is a corporation with obligations to the franchisor that the corporation cannot fulfill, then by virtue of personally guaranteeing those obligations, you'll be responsible for fulfilling these obligations on behalf of the corporation to the franchisor. If this is a problem, sometimes the franchisor will be willing to cap the personal guarantee so that at the very least (if you are concerned about exposing your personal assets), you may be able to negotiate a cap or limit to the personal guarantee. Keep in mind that the franchisor is entering this relationship as you are with every intent for success and what they are attempting to do is protect themselves in the event of any problems. You may also be asked to sign a noncompete provision, which protects the franchisor from your breaking away or leaving the franchise and setting up as a competitor, utilizing the know-how and the proprietary information that you were provided as a franchisee.

Once again, if you bring a certain amount of knowledge and know-how to this franchise, there may be some ways that certain noncompete provisions can be negotiated; however, this tends to get very sticky and requires a very knowledgeable franchise attorney to help guide you down that path. Generally, franchisors will not negotiate a noncompete.

When it came to personal guarantees and noncompetes, I never took anyone's home away even though I had some franchisees that had committed some egregious acts. All we basically wanted was to be made financially whole. I can't speak for every franchisor in America, but I do know that in my experience—and I think in the case of most franchisors—they simply want to protect themselves and are after the same result that you are: a successful franchise in a particular market or territory.

If this process has been completed and you've made a positive decision, then the next step would be to receive the contracts and agreements from the franchisor for you and your attorney's final review. You must receive the final copies of the franchise agreement to be executed at least five (5) business days before signing. This gives you a period of time so that you can review these documents and consider your decision. So, remember that you are afforded some rights in that regard.

On the other hand, if based upon the visit that you make and the results of that visit you decide not to choose that particular franchise, then sometimes the best decision is not to go forward. Over the years, I've learned that some of the best deals are the ones I walked away from. This is a very important step in your life and you will be investing your money and devoting a good deal of your time, attention, and resources to this franchise. If there is any doubt in your mind that you don't believe you will be successful or certain items you requested weren't granted, then perhaps the best decision for you is not to proceed.

Now that you have completed that key process, the next step is to negotiate the agreement and plan to open your business. It's very critical that you develop a business plan for your new franchise. The benefit of owning a franchise is that you already know what the ingredients for success are.

During my career, I always followed the credo that it's one thing to develop a plan or program, yet another to execute it. After all, whether it's business or any other endeavor, it's performance that makes the difference between the winners and the losers. As you create your business plan, you need to keep this fact in mind. It's the execution that makes the difference.

You will need a good business plan to set forth your objectives and for any financial resources you'll need. Your chances to obtain credit lines or additional working capital will be supported by a good comprehensive business plan. If you want some tips on writing a business plan, you can obtain guidance from the "bookstore" or on the "Internet." In any case, you'll want to be sure that your business plan include the following attributes:

1. Statement of Purpose—This is your introductory section. It's here that the person reading the business plan will understand what your business objectives are and what you seek from others.
2. Business Description—You will describe your business and the industry in which you operate. This will give the readers the opportunity to understand what products or services your business will offer.

3. Business Strategy—How will you develop and market your business? What are the markets you will sell or service? What is the competitive environment you'll be operating in and how will your business be able to overcome these factors?

4. Financial Presentation—This is a very important element of your business plan. The preceding components will lead into what your financial goals and details are. You should have a pro forma income statement, balance sheets, and cash flow statements. As you seek financial assistance, this section of your business plan will receive the most scrutiny.

To be effective, a business plan need not look like the work of an Ivy League MBA. Rather, it should be concise, factual, and realistic. A good rule of thumb is to show your business plan draft to a qualified friend or advisor and ask them to objectively critique it. In addition to utilizing a business plan for financing purposes, it allows you to construct a roadmap for your business.

All businesses require a cash flow projection. The cash flow projection is a necessary ingredient for success, for being able to identify what your cash flow needs are and to measure the performance of your business from a cash flow standpoint on a regular basis. Some small business owners may have a budget, and it might even be information that they carry in their head; nevertheless, they know what they need to acheive in terms of sales and profits in order to meet the expenses that they have and hopefully earn a profit at the end of each week or month.

It goes without saying that having a cash flow statement will require you to make projections on expenses as well as on sales and on the profitability on those sales. As is so often the case, if you don't know where you are going, then obviously any road will lead you there. It's very important to have a plan and a budget so that you're able to understand what your requirements are and what the results will be based upon reaching certain levels of sales and expenses. As you are in the process of getting ready to acquire and start your franchise, you will need to do a cash flow projection. You'll need to set forth your estimated sales, gross margin, and expenses in order to identify your cash flow process and see at what levels of sales, profits, and expenses your business will be either generating cash or expending cash. If you don't follow the process, you could end up being in the position of having acquired a franchise and starting a new business without fully having your financial targets and goals put together.

Following are examples of a pro forma income statement and cash flow projection. There are spreadsheets available on line, which can be downloaded to your computer. Some sites may or may not charge a small fee.

Pro Forma
Income Statement

	Jan	Feb	Mar	Apr	May	June	July	Aug	Sept	Oct	Nov	Dec
Sales												
Gross Margin												
Expenses:												
Rent												
Payroll												
Officers' Salaries												
Benefits												
Withholding taxes												
Telephone												
Advertising												
Supplies												
Utilities												
Insurance												
Travel/Entertain.												
Professional fees												
Interest Expense												
Amortization/ Depreciation												
Other Expenses												
Total Expenses:												
Pre-tax Profit												
Taxes												
Net Profit after Taxes												

Cash Flow Projection

	Jan	Feb	Mar	Apr	May	June	July	Aug	Sept	Oct	Nov	Dec
Cash:												
Net income												
A/P income												
N/P income												
Liabilities income												
Long term debt												
Other												
Total Cash												
Cash Outflow:												
A/P decrease												
N/P decrease												
Decrease in long-term debt												
Shareholder div.												
Other												
Total Cash Flow												
Monthly cash Flow												
Cumulative												

I would encourage you to use the franchisor for information and advice in terms of the ingredients that you will include in your cash flow. I don't think it's unreasonable to expect the franchisor to provide you with the very best information regarding expenses in terms of what a typical rental might be based upon your space needs. What kind of staffing levels or employees you will need to hire. What kind of costs you will incur in advertising, etc. Any reliable franchisor should provide you with that information. You can use that in combination with what you feel your sales projection will be and the profits on those sales.

My advice to franchisees over the years has always been to put a plan together and then ask yourself, based upon your analysis of market conditions, your capability and your financial resources, whether you feel as a franchisee, you can achieve the results set forth in the plan. That is after all, the objective of having a good cash flow projection or statement. Projections are a necessary part of all businesses, from the standpoint of starting the business to ongoing management. Without a cash flow projection, you'll have no way to know how profitable your business might be or how profitable it can be based upon certain expenses and sales results. In order to make an intelligent business decision, you need to have a cash flow statement and you need to know exactly what the results are based upon the performance you achieve.

Whether you go into the detail of devising a business plan as I had suggested, I feel it's imperative that you have a cash flow statement which will serve, not only as a portrait of your financial situation, but will also provide you the basis of a budget. It's very important that you have this kind of information so that you can follow and track your performance. Once you put together your cash flow statement, I think it is imperative that you let the franchisor, in particular, the individuals whom you have been working with, take a look at it. This does not imply that your failure to achieve these results will place any responsibility on the part of the franchisor, but I think it makes a great deal of sense to see how they feel about your cash flow projection. I was always impressed with those franchisees that put together a cash flow projection and asked for my comments and the comments of those who worked for me. It clearly indicated to me that they had business savvy and recognized the importance of setting forth a plan that would put "pen to paper" so to speak, the numbers, which they had to achieve.

Having a well-thought-out and sensible cash flow projection is important for all businesses and it is extremely important for you, as you are about to embark on your new franchise opportunity.

CHAPTER 5

Negotiating the Franchise Agreement

*Once everything is put together, you'll be left
with a document that you will be held to for the
duration of your franchise.*

Now that you have decided on the franchise that you want
to buy, the next step is to finalize your franchise agreement. You
and your attorney will need to work together so that both of you
are comfortable with the agreement that you'll be signing. After
you've identified those sections or provisions of the agreement
that you feel are problematic, the next step is to present this
information to the franchisor.

Be advised that some franchisors will not make changes in
their franchise agreement, while others may be more willing to
negotiate certain changes.

For example, *Marc Shuman*, CEO of Garage Tek a franchisor
located in Syosset, New York, does not negotiate the franchise
agreement. He states, "I take somewhat of an aggressive approach
regarding the franchise agreement and any attempt to negotiate
terms. I want my franchisees to be held to the same standards

and want to have each agreement to be identical." Also, Shuman only provides the UFOC during the first face-to-face meeting and does not send it out through the mail. He advises the prospective franchisee to have a franchise attorney to thoroughly review the agreement as opposed to a friend or advisor. His practice regarding the process of distributing and negotiating the franchise agreement is in no way unique and will be found among many franchisors.

On the other hand, *Jeff Bernstein*, CEO of Trufood Corp., will mail a UFOC to a prospective franchisee if that person has been well qualified. Bernstein also adds, "We do exercise some limited flexibility to negotiate certain terms of the franchise agreement excluding the royalty, length of term, termination provisions to name a few." As you can see, there are differences among franchisors when it comes to making changes to their franchise agreement. Recall my advice in chapter 3, you should ask the question of what is negotiable early on in the process so that you and your attorney are prepared for the negotiating process.

Assuming that the franchisor you're working with is willing to discuss some changes to their franchise agreement, then I would suggest that you go into the process of negotiating this agreement with an open-mind. Keep in mind that the quality of the franchise and the relationship between the franchisor and the franchisees that you have already spoken to will help determine in part how aggressive you will be in negotiating the agreement. The old expression in business is that "when you agree to something, get it in writing in the event someone gets run over by the proverbial truck." So, any good businessperson will always want to make sure that anything that has been agreed upon is memorialized in writing whether it's within the franchise agreement itself or in the form of an amendment to the agreement. The other important reason for making sure that everything is in writing rather than relying on verbal commitments or promises is that franchise agreements contain a provision that in laymen's terms basically says, "If it is not part of the agreement and in writing then it's invalid." The reason for that is to protect the franchisor since someone may come back and make accusations or statements that the franchisee was promised something that was not in the agreement. It will also serve to protect the franchisee because it is a warning. It's an acknowledgment that you had better get it in writing because if you don't, it will not take effect. There may also be a disclaimer of earnings with the acknowledgment of receipt. The important point is to make sure that you go through your negotiations and ultimately achieve the document you and your attorney feel comfortable with. You should make sure that you have everything in writing, so that you will have the comfort level you need.

There are different styles in negotiating the franchise agreement. There are those who would prefer to negotiate through their attorney, where the attorney would be in direct contact with certain individuals at the franchisor headquarters. The other approach is where the attorney would communicate through the franchise candidate. I found, quite frankly, that it was most effective when I dealt with the franchise candidate and if there were issues that seemed a little difficult to deal with, then I might deal with their attorney. I was rather fortunate in that I had a significant amount of experience in franchising and would not have to get our corporate counsel involved in negotiating terms of the franchise agreement except in some rare instances. Generally, I was in a position where I would be able to discuss those few open items or issues with the franchisee candidate's attorney, and just about in every case, I was able to work things out.

Your approach in dealing with any negotiations should be to include your attorney. In other words, you could negotiate with the franchisor or with the franchisor representative and always have the ability to comment that you need to run it past your attorney just to make sure everything is okay. I must confess that in my career, those franchisees that were the most challenging from a negotiating standpoint who were ultimately able to get what they wanted typically would negotiate themselves and then go back to their attorney to make sure everything met with their approval.

I have to say that in a rather humorous vein, I can recall some candidates who would tell me that everything was done. I thought everything was worked out and then just when I thought I was going to get the deal signed, they would say, "I just have to run it past my attorney." I often wondered if they actually had an attorney, and even if they did, it makes me wonder if they were using the attorney as a foil. Many times, they would come back and say, "There is just one more item my attorney feels that I need." I would suggest that you may be better off to speak with the franchisor and you could bounce any issues or problems off your attorney. If you are dealing with a large franchisor, they may have in-house legal counsel who would deal with your attorney directly.

The kinds of items and the changes in the agreement that you want are going to be very important. As I stated previously, once everything is put together, you'll be left with a document that you will be held to for the duration of your franchise. It is very difficult to have a franchisor go back and make a change in the agreement. In fact, it's near impossible! Sometimes, the best you can hope for is some concession, but it probably is not going to be in writing because a franchisor is reluctant to go back and change the agreement after it has already been agreed to. I would not take this entire exercise lightly since it is probably the most important component of the relationship. It's the final and key step in putting everything together. Recognize that the franchisor must have a strong agreement and must be careful that they aren't granting concessions to franchisees that could come back to haunt them. Having this understanding as a franchise candidate is extremely important and your attorney must share that feeling as well.

This does not say that you should never walk away from an agreement or a deal. In fact, if you or your attorney don't feel comfortable with the terms of the agreement or feel that there is unreasonable resistance on the part of the franchisor to address some of your most simple requests, then I think you have to start questioning the franchisor. If they are unreasonable before you begin, it could be more difficult later on. Keep in mind that the larger franchisor is in the position where they don't have to concede very much in the form of negotiations. Also, the larger franchisor has to be very careful because they can grant a concession to a franchisee that, quite frankly, could have an impact throughout their entire franchise system.

One of the comments that I've often heard from franchisees and their attorneys is that the franchise agreement is "one-sided" in favor of the franchisor. Whenever this has come up, my response is that the franchise agreement is in fact somewhat one-sided. However, it has to be. If you don't have a strong franchise agreement, then you can't have a strong franchise system. The franchisor needs to have a strong agreement in order to enforce the standards throughout the franchise system. Just imagine that you bought a franchise and invested your hard-earned money in growing that business only to find that a franchisee in another section of town or in an adjoining city or state is doing a very poor job. This can result in damage or harm to the brand name of the franchise and you. That franchisee, not only impacts your ability to be able to grow and prosper, but the ability of other franchisees. A poor performing franchisee hurts not only themselves and the franchisor but also probably more than any other group, his or her fellow franchisees. That is why experienced franchise executives and franchisees recognize that a strong franchise agreement protects the good franchisees from the bad. So, when you look at a franchise agreement and your attorney comes back and reports that this is very one-sided, keep these points in mind. Of course, you should still give the franchisor the opportunity to respond to any issues you have with the agreement.

If you follow the advice that I have given you regarding the review of the franchise agreement and the UFOC and use capable franchise counsel, you will be in a good position to fully understand the terms of the agreement, and when necessary, negotiate those terms that you feel are important. I have dealt with countless attorneys representing franchisees, and in some cases, attorneys not well versed in franchising. Some franchisees incurred additional costs because their attorney negotiated certain provisions of the franchise agreement that were not very important. All of this because their attorney did not understand and were not experienced in franchising. My advice is to make sure you use an attorney that has an understanding of franchising. They do not have to be a world expert, but they should have had some experience in dealing with franchise agreements so that they can give you sound advice and, when items are negotiated, assist you accordingly.

Be sure to ask the attorney you intend to use if they have reviewed and negotiated franchise agreements. With regard to negotiating the franchise agreement, my advice is the best time for this is during the face-to-face meeting at the franchisor's corporate headquarters. You can bring it up at that point or you can communicate to the franchisor's salesperson prior to your meeting, indicating that you have some items that you would like to negotiate. The bottom line is that most franchisors are willing to listen and some will negotiate parts of the franchise agreement. However, I would always tell franchisees that I had a certain set of rules when it comes to the franchise agreement. Many franchisors may follow the same format.

My rules worked this way:
1. There are "non-negotiable items." These are the royalties, the initial franchise fee, the territory, the length or term of the agreement, termination provisions, and venue. I would not negotiate a change to these items.
2. Certain legal provisions in the agreement were subject to negotiation and change if it could be done in a way that did not materially alter the agreement. Some franchisors have strong franchise agreements so it is a given that some prospective franchisees and/or their attorneys will bring up some of these issues and would want to negotiate them.

3. There were certain business items that I was willing to negotiate. Some of these may include a provision for advertising expenditures on a monthly or annual basis. You might request some other changes and I believe many franchisors will consider negotiating the business components of the franchise agreement. These aren't the "non-negotiable items" or the legal provisions, and some may be willing to negotiate these points.

My rule of thumb was that if I negotiated something with one franchisee and another franchisee said that they wanted the same thing, I was comfortable in doing that. If the change would not impair our ability to administer the system and enforce the standards of the program and uphold the agreements. That is why I had the so-called "non-negotiable items" that I would not negotiate. Moreover, I did not want to have a situation where I had a group of franchisees paying different royalties. Not only is it unfair, but also discriminatory.

The last rule that I followed was that I would never insist on anything that diminished or reduced the rights of the franchisee. Anything that I negotiated would be a benefit to them, and in some cases, these benefits were minor yet important to the new franchisee. These were my rules and that was the creed that I followed when negotiating agreements. You will find most franchisors willing to listen to the concerns of you and your attorney. Just keep in mind that the larger franchisors may be reluctant and unable to agree to as many changes to their franchise agreement as those who are just starting up or in the early stages of growth. By the way, during my career I have encountered attorneys who negotiated from the UFOC instead of the franchise agreement itself. Remember, it is the franchise agreement that represents the contract you sign. Therefore, it's important that any negotiation relates specifically to the provisions within the franchise agreement as opposed to descriptions that exist in the UFOC section.

Following are some suggestions regarding items you may wish to negotiate or at the very least obtain some clarification in writing:

Be careful not to ask for too much. If the agreement is that onerous, then perhaps this franchise is not for you. On the other hand, many franchisors will turn down a potential franchisee rather than agree to a laundry list of demands. My suggestion is that you negotiate only those points that will be important to you during your franchise ownership. Ultimately, you and your attorney will make the final decision.

Preamble—If you have any questions regarding the services or products that you'll provide under the franchise agreement, be sure these are answered or clarified. You may be unsure if you can sell or market certain products or services. Now is the time to clarify any issues.

Territory—There may be open territory adjoining the franchise territory you seek. Perhaps you can service or market that territory until it's franchised. You will not be allowed to open a location there; however, you might be able to market in this open area. Another suggestion is to ask for a right of first refusal. Many franchisees look for an opportunity to acquire additional territory or another franchise if the one they acquire is successful. If you truly desire to have an additional franchise, you can request the franchisor to give you a "right of first refusal" which in its simplest terms provides you an opportunity to acquire another franchise or territory if the franchisor receives a bona fide offer from another party for the same territory. However, be advised that many franchisors deny these requests since it could cost them a qualified franchise if the person having the right of first refusal turns down the opportunity after taking time to make a decision. It can also cause some resentment on the part of the franchisee holding the right of first refusal since a qualified candidate may appear before the existing franchisee is prepared to acquire another franchise.

If you are able to obtain a right of first refusal, be prepared to pay a nonrefundable deposit and/or have very little time to exercise your right, sign a franchise agreement, and pay the full franchise fee.

Over the years, my recommendation to a new franchisee is to maximize the territory and opportunity that they have and not to dilute their effectiveness by taking on more than they can handle from a financial as well as operational standpoint.

Mergers and Acquisitions—If the agreement has a provision, which allows the franchisor to acquire a similar business and operate within your territory, request the option to acquire this business upon the same terms as the franchisor. At the very least, be sure the franchisor can't make this type of acquisition and use the franchise marks to compete against your franchise within your own territory. Be sure you and your attorney fully understand the "exclusivity" nature of your franchise.

Renewal Terms—some renewal provisions require the franchisee to execute a release for all claims against the franchisor. This is an opportunity when you do renew to "clean up" any old issues. You may request language to exclude certain "open items" from the release. Additionally, you can request that the franchisor release you from claims, which may have taken place prior to your renewal term. Be careful regarding upgrades and remodels so that this provision can't be used against you. Keep in mind that a full release from any claims against the franchisor for the period prior to the renewal will prevent you from seeking recourse in the event there are any unresolved items or issues.

Royalty Payments—Don't expect any change here. Remember, this is one of the "non-negotiable items."

Additional Products and Services Royalty—If you have a question or potential conflict regarding certain products or service royalties, get them clarified now. Don't wait until you've signed the franchise agreement and then have a problem. This may fall into the category of certain franchise programs whereby the franchisee may be in the position of selling certain services or products outside the terms of this franchise agreement.

Advertising—If there is a minimum advertising requirement, you may wish to request a reduction for your first year. Sections which require you to submit all advertising for franchisor approval might require clarification. If approval is required, be sure you receive a quick response from the franchisor so you don't have to wait an unreasonable period of time. Provisions regarding your mandatory participation in an "advertising fund" ought to be carefully reviewed by your attorney. You should request a copy of meeting minutes or program guidelines to review. Be sure to verify whether or not your franchisor will participate or contribute to a "grand opening" program. Provisions where the franchisor requires franchisees to advertise in the yellow pages should be reviewed. Yellow page display ads can be very costly, so make sure you understand your obligations. Internet advertising and Web site must be fully understood. Determine if you can post your own Web site, and if yes, is it subject to franchisor review and approval? This is an important area for possible growth depending upon the nature of the franchise business.

Site Selection Requirements—Since you'll pay the rent for the location, be sure that you have a full understanding as to your obligations under the terms of the franchise agreement. Be sure your attorney carefully checks this section, and if necessary, you ought to request changes.

Modifications to the System—Most franchise agreements have provisions, which allow the franchisor to modify certain terms of the franchise agreement via the operations manual. This type of provision can be onerous to a franchisee. You may wish to have language, whereby changes to the franchise agreement or operations manual cannot materially increase your financial obligations.

Financial Statements—Be prepared to submit the financial information that you are required to provide the franchisor under this section. You need to understand the difference between audited, certified, and a compilation of financial statements.

Covenants not to Compete—If you have an issue here, "speak now or forever hold your peace." This is one of the "non-negotiable items." Don't expect changes here.

Indemnification—The franchise agreement may require the franchisee to indemnify the franchisor regardless of whether or not a loss is the fault of the franchisee. This section requires careful scrutiny since it could hold the franchisee responsible for reimbursing the franchisor regardless of the cause. Your attorney can request to "soften" this type of language by inserting something to the effect "provided that claims under this provision are not the responsibility of the franchisee when the franchisee followed the policy and procedures of the franchisor."

Minimum Performance Requirement—This type of section should be responsible and equitable. You don't want to be in a position where you performed well for several years and then as a result of factors beyond your control you are subject to termination. Be sure that you fully understand your responsibilities if this provision is in your franchise agreement.

Assignment and Transfers—This section will deal with the sale and assignment of your franchise. The franchisor will always have a right of first refusal, which will allow the franchisor to match any offer for the purchase of your franchise. Your attorney should carefully review this section. Some franchisors may allow some changes to this section. You want to be sure that the franchisor cannot unreasonably withhold consent to an assignment. Also, you may wish to negotiate the time lines for the assignment (sale) process. If the franchisor has a period of sixty (60) or ninety (90) days to exercise their rights, you could lose your buyer. Keep in mind that this section may be much more important to you than it is to the franchisor. Don't be reluctant to request changes.

Termination—This is one of the most important provisions in your franchise agreement. Some franchise agreements contain three termination categories: Automatic termination without notice; termination upon notice with no opportunity to cure; and termination with a cure period.

Your must have your attorney review the termination section so that you will fully understand what the termination provisions are. You don't want to face losing your franchise due to a lack of understanding on your part. Most franchisors are unwilling to make changes to the termination section and for good reason. Changes on behalf of particular franchisees and not others could lead to problems for the franchisor. If you or your attorney are unable to make changes to this section, you may opt to have certain sections clarified. This will provide you answers to those questions you may have.

I hope you are successful in negotiating, or at least being comfortable with this section of your agreement. Remember, once you execute your franchise agreement, you have agreed to comply with all of its terms.

Although there are other provisions to your franchise agreement, the ones in this chapter are the most noteworthy. Be sure your attorney gives you a level of comfort so that your signature is anxiety free.

CHAPTER 6

Opening your Franchise

*The first 3 months of your new franchise
are the most critical.*

Now that you have signed your franchise documents, the next step is opening your new franchise business. Franchisors typically provide either a "New Opening Guide" or a section in their operations manual, which details the key steps for a new location opening. Up until this point in time, you've spent your efforts on evaluating the franchise opportunity, meeting the franchisor and negotiating your franchise agreement. Now, it's time to take action in order to get your new business operational!

From this moment on, you will start to expend significant time and capital on your new business. The start-up phase of a new business is important since most small business fail within the first year, with the first 3-6 months being the critical time frame. Having the support of a franchise system provides an advantage over an independent business; nevertheless, you'll still need to generate sales and profits to succeed. Remember, that there is no guarantee of success simply because you're part of a franchise operation.

You should already have your cash flow projections, which will serve as your budget, and financial guidelines you will need to follow. Depending upon the type of franchise you operate, the location can be very important to your success. When I worked with a large retail franchisor, our criteria were the usual three (3) factors for success—location, location, and location. In another instance, I was with a service franchisor where the location was much less important.

If your franchise is a retail or food business format, then the franchisor should have a good deal of information and will provide strong support and guidance in the area of site location. Chances are, you already have several locations in mind and may have already discussed those with the franchisor before you executed your franchise agreement.

This is also a good time to introduce yourself to the more successful franchisees in your geographic area. Tell them that you just acquired a franchise and you have a few questions to ask. I don't care how many manuals and checklists you follow; it's in the real world where "things" happen. You have the opportunity to gain advice and guidance from the franchisor as well as some of the franchisees. Be sure that you have all of your activities carefully programmed and especially the following:

1. How much support does the franchise provide during preopening, grand opening, and postopening? Don't take anything for granted; rather, make sure training is scheduled and onsite support, if provided, is planned.
2. Have a new opening checklist available for your opening. Implement advertising plans.
3. Have your employees hired and ready to start, when needed.
4. Plan on obtaining "PR" for your grand opening.

Here is some information you can utilize to assist with opening your new franchise:

Market Analysis

One of the most important ingredients of running a successful business is to know your competition. The services they provide, how they provide those services and their strengths and weaknesses. Knowledge of your competition helps you position yourself strategically in the market. Obtaining information about your competitors and the manner in which they do business has become a vital source of information by which companies market their products. This practice has long become an integral part of sophisticated marketing programs. It is smart business.

Market analysis is a means of gathering important information about your market competitors. It gives you some insight into the quality and techniques of your competitor. Be sure to conduct your market analysis before you open your location. Initially, you should try to understand what your market conditions are:

1. Who are your competitors?
2. What is their pricing?
3. Estimated revenue.
4. How do they advertise and where?
5. Obtain any of their marketing literature for review.
6. What is the approximate size of the market that you are in?
7. What are the perceived strengths and weaknesses of your competitors?

There are many other resources available such as the Internet. The Internet can give you an overview of your competitor's services, products, locations, etc. You can gather this information without having to leave your computer.

Identification of Competition

Company Name	Years in Business	Market Share	Specialization

Perceived Strength and Weakness
of the Competition

Company	Strengths	Weakness

Internal Strengths and Weaknesses Worksheet

Strengths	Weaknesses

Your Professional Advice

It is most important that you have an accountant, attorney, and an insurance agent who are competent and interested in your success. If you use someone that you are not familiar with, be sure that you get a referral from someone that you can trust. Depending upon the size of the business in which you will be initially involved, you may not wish to engage larger firms. You're much better off with small- to medium-sized firms where you will be a significant client. If on the other hand, your plans are to open a very large franchise operation, then that's a whole different matter.

Insurance Agent

The insurance requirements of your business, in many respects, may be quite unique. Be sure you have sufficient protection. Your franchisor should have insurance coverage requirements or guidelines. In most cases, this information is included in your franchise agreement or operations manual.

Attorney

After your business is established, you will probably have little ongoing need for your attorney. Most of the attorney's activity will take place prior to and during the formative stages of your business. You will need your attorney to (1) register your business with local authorities and (2) form a corporation. Under a corporate structure, it is the attorney's responsibility to set up your corporate minutes book, prepare the stock certificates, order your corporate seal, and prepare whatever documentation and materials are required for your corporation to be legally constituted. If on the other hand, your business is a partnership, you may want the attorney to draw up a partnership agreement. Be sure you have an attorney who has franchise experience in case you require assistance in the future.

Accountant

Although your franchisor may provide you with different weekly, monthly, quarterly, or annual management financial reports, the accounting and tax returns for your office should be done by your own accountant. It is important that you have your accountant set up your system of books, records, and financial reports.

Hiring Your Staff

A key ingredient in the development of a successful franchise business is the staff you hire.

Some key attributes to look for in your staff:

1. Communication Skills
   - Listen effectively
   - Use appropriate vocabulary
   - Respond clearly and directly
   - Be articulate

2. Organization Ability
   - Handle filing and reporting
   - Be able to establish schedules, meet deadlines, and understand
   - Territorial management
   - Maintain effectiveness, composure, and flexibility under pressure
   - Plan and complete assignments on time

3. Interpersonal Skills
   - Work effectively with a variety of individuals
   - Reorganize strengths and limitations in self and others
   - Gain confidence and trust of others
   - Exhibit tenacity
   - Interface with applicants, prospects, and clients

4. Assertiveness and Enthusiasm
   - Maintain high energy level, be persistent and eager
   - Enjoy challenges and responsibility
   - Communicate in a positive and constructive manner

The above are what I consider to be the key attributes that you should consider when you hire your staff. Obviously, the various strengths and importance of these attributes will vary depending upon the exact type of business that you are starting.

In order to insure success, we must also be able to profile the individual who has a potential for failure. No matter how great the person looks or how impressive they appear on paper, the following are examples of factors that can inhibit an individual's effective performance:

Reasons Not to Select an Applicant

Don't hire:

> Someone with no business or sales experience.
> A shy person.
> A person with a poor telephone voice.
> Someone who demonstrates poor judgment.
> Someone who does not appear to be flexible.
> A person with a fear of rejection.
> A person who must take a major cut in pay.
> A person with a nonbusiness-like attitude or appearance.
> A person who is not a team player.
> A person who cannot account for long periods of unemployment.
> A person whose application does not cross-reference with his or her resume.
> A person who projects a negative attitude toward former employers.
> A person who has held too many positions in too short a period of time.
> A friend or a relative unless you have truly thought it through.

In terms of where you would recruit your employees, I would suggest that you advertise in your local newspaper. If you are seeking individuals with sales experience, you may want to place the ad in the section of the newspaper where the proper individuals seeking that type of employment can read it. Depending upon the size and scope of your business, you may wish to utilize the Internet. This will depend upon the type of individuals you are seeking. I would be very careful, depending upon the type of individual you are seeking to hire, to be sure you are spending the appropriate funds. These are some very useful tips in terms of you recruiting and interviewing candidates. Be sure that if you do in fact narrow your choices down to one or two candidates, that you give them the appropriate information regarding the position so that you don't have any misunderstandings or problems when they are hired. It is very important to remember that the individuals you hire in your business can very well make or break your business. They can make a difference between success and failure.

The Interview Process

It is not my intent to review all the points of an interview, but to cover the basic flow of events that occur when interviewing and hiring personnel. When interviewing, do not inadvertently start a line of questioning that will be inappropriate. Restrict your questions to those qualifying the person to the position. Do not ask questions relating to race, creed, color, religion, age, sexual preference or orientation, sex, national origin physical or mental handicap, ancestry, marital status, military status, or for any other grounds prohibited by local law. Your franchisor may have some information regarding this area. In any case, be sure you conduct yourself accordingly.

The Interview

Once you have invited a prospective candidate for an initial interview, be prepared to spend sufficient time to interview and evaluate the candidate and be sure the candidate completes an application prior to the interview.

Briefly explain the purpose of the interview:

• Gain information about the applicant
• Explore appropriateness of the job for the applicant
• Explore previous background
• Provide a job description

- Answer questions
- Mutual agreement on whether or not to explore the position further

There are a few simple steps to let the applicant know what will happen during the interview. Putting him or her at ease will increase your chances of obtaining maximum information and establishing a professional relationship and image.

Gathering Information

You should begin by getting the basics out of the way. Conduct a full interview, using the application form as a guide. Then move on to exploring those questions that reveal both basic qualities and selection standard profiles.

Ask open-ended questions, digging deeper when you need more information. An open-ended question is one that can't be answered by a simple yes or no.

In asking open-ended questions, keep control of the interview. If the applicant starts to ramble, bring the conversation back to where it's giving you the information you need. On the other hand, don't be afraid of using silence. If you ask important questions and don't get an answer, wait the applicant out. That way you don't end up putting an answer in the applicant's mouth.

Giving Information

The next phase of the interview allows the candidate to alleviate some of the stress you have built up during information gathering. This is where you present details of the position, benefits, etc. It also sets the stage for further interviews and, if a good match occurs, it sets the stage for the candidate's eventual acceptance of the job.

Potential Employee Evaluation

The final phase of the interview is to evaluate the candidate. Are you favorably impressed enough to pursue this applicant?

If after the interview your evaluation is positive and you feel this person is a potential candidate, arrange for them to return for a second interview. If you do not think a match exists, send the applicant a "thank you for your interest" letter.

In either case, you have two objectives:

One: To increase your odds in selecting and eventually hiring the best candidate.

Two: To create a positive image. A rejected candidate may become an applicant, a client, or a source for referrals in the future.

References

Assuming that you have positive results in the evaluation process, your next step would be to check at least two references. This step is often overlooked only to have negative information or behavior surface after the hire is complete. It is much wiser to invest a half-hour up front than to risk time and training.

Most companies are reluctant to go into much detail on former employees, so you will have to create a climate that will encourage them to be honest with you.

It may be necessary to obtain written referrals. Remember you need the candidate's specific permission in order to do so. This permission also applies to credit or character checks of any nature.

The Offer

If you are confident that this applicant is a match for your office, offer them the position. If an offer is made and accepted, discuss the details of employment.

Setting Up Your Location

In order to facilitate opening your business you need to follow the guidelines that your franchisor provides. Most franchisors have specific requirements or instructions for location, decor, equipment, etc. Every franchisor that I have been affiliated with provided a grand opening package, whether they provide you some materials as I did with several of my franchise companies or they give you guidelines or various resources to include a grand opening package. You will usually be provided with some guidance as to how to establish a grand opening for your business

Grand Opening

To announce your business opening, there are certain contacts you want to make. Your Chamber of Commerce should be contacted and consider joining this association. It is a good opportunity to make valuable contacts. A successful grand opening campaign involves a significant amount of time and effort. It requires, and is dependent on, the implementation of a variety of effective marketing activities including advertising, public relations, direct mail, and sales promotion. It also demands carefully planned grand opening kick-off events. Your franchisor should have a grand opening campaign for you to follow, however, just in case I've listed some important items.

- Your business generating/sales presentations should begin as soon as you have a location, telephone, and the staff to handle customers and service inquiries/requests.
- Distribution of a general press release to local media announcing your grand opening. I would recommend directing press releases to the community at large. Placing it in a variety of publications so that customers, potential employees, and other members of the community will see it. Most publications/newspapers, etc. will be more than willing to put a sample press release in their local paper. If you are dealing with an extremely large newspaper such as the *Boston Globe* and the *New York Times,* it might be a little more difficult, but I am sure in your local community you will find some print media that will accommodate you.

- Implementation of an ongoing campaign to attract business. This should reflect your activities to announce, not only your new business but to also attract new customers or clients.
- Make sure you have developed recruiting and business generating sales strategies so that your business is ready to go. Of course, depending upon the type of business that you're involved in, your activities will vary. The important thing is that you are prepared and you recognize that your grand opening event is an open house. It's a gathering of people who constitute the key members of your community and marketplace. It should also represent an opportunity to attract new customers.
- Initiation of business generating sales, utilizing applicable brochures, advertising, and a marketing plan.
- Press release should be issued. If your franchisor doesn't provide sample press releases, there are numerous examples you can draw from company Web sites.

Grand Opening Event

The grand opening event is an open house. It is a gathering of people who constitute your referring community.

The open house provides an ideal forum for you and your staff to develop the professional associations necessary for your franchise's location success. It gives you and those who attend (people with the potential to refer business to you) the opportunity to learn about each other: You will learn about potential clients' specific needs and expectations; potential clients will learn how you can effectively meet the requirements of the community. The open house event will be held at your location. This gives you the opportunity to highlight your new business, its furnishings and equipment, systems and of course, your professional and enthusiastic staff.

Planning the Event

An effective open house event requires significant promotion and preparation. Careful planning in advance will enable you and your staff to enjoy this special day.

- Promotion: effective promotion of the open house requires two main activities—direct mail and personal contact. It takes time to research and develop a comprehensive invitation list. Since your objective is to invite as many targeted people as possible, the effort will be worth it. This will also tie into your general development of a prospect list and an announcement list. In addition, look in the Government Blue Pages of your White Pages Directory to locate public officials. Having dignitaries attend will add credibility to your event and maximize the chance of having it covered by the press. Be sure to invite the

  - mayor / deputy mayor
  - assembly members
  - director, state's employment / unemployment office

These names can be kept in your computer for future follow-up. Keep a list of all those who attend so that follow-up thank-you notes can be written.

Also, try to get particularly well-known and respected individuals to attend your open house. An example might be an educator, politician, sports figure, radio personality, music or television star, etc. If a celebrity agrees to attend, play it up! Use his or her name in appropriate communications. This may increase your exposure in the media resulting in an even better turnout at your event.

- Telephone contact: Shortly after your invitations have been mailed, you should visit or call the individuals on your list and let them know that an invitation is on its way.

- When promoting your event, don't overlook the media. Most cities/towns have newspapers and local/cable news station focusing on local happenings. Invite writers, business editors, consumer editors, reporters, and photographers.

Your franchisor should have all of the tools necessary to get you started. That is one of the benefits of being a franchisee!

CHAPTER 7

Leadership and Motivation

Respect, feedback, understanding, and
recognition are the positive factors.

Although this book is devoted primarily to franchising, I would be remiss if I did not include a chapter on business management. I've entitled this particular chapter Leadership and Motivation. The content is based upon what I feel are the two most important ingredients in effective business management. When we consider the great CEOs of American business, the names Alfred Sloan, Tom Watson, and Jack Welch are usually mentioned. However, I believe that there are vital aspects of leadership and motivation that are practiced by business people throughout the United States every day of the year.

After having spent over thirty years in business, most of which were spent in management or supervisory positions, I've had the ability to learn a great deal about leadership and motivation, not only from personal experience, but also from having studied a good deal about the subject. Based upon this, I've established my own set of principles pertaining to leadership and motivation.

One of the unique attributes of American business is that we often use money or wealth as the ultimate measure of success. We often consider those individuals who have been fortunate enough through hard work, good timing, intelligence, and creativity to possess certain traits and qualities that rise above and beyond the average businessperson.

As an example, Donald Trump has accumulated a great deal of wealth and success. Certainly, Mr. Trump would quite naturally be considered an effective leader and motivator; however, it doesn't necessarily follow that his particular performance in leading and motivating is better than that of a department manager that may be supervising eight people. The point is we sometimes consider those who have achieved a certain level of material or organizational success as being in possession of great leadership and motivational skills. This is not always the case, since certainly, some individuals might be placed in a particular position because of the right timing, and a confluence of events, etc. Not to deny them their due, but it doesn't mean that other managers don't possess those same traits of leadership and motivation.

When I discuss leadership and motivational skills, I think about certain principles that I have followed throughout my career that have served as the foundation of how I conduct myself in leading and motivating my subordinates. I shall define these principles as the "positive factors." They are respect, feedback, understanding, and recognition. I will define each one and then present what I consider to be the "negative factors" or opposites of the positive leadership and motivational traits.

By "respect," I refer to every individual being treated fairly, whatever his or her position in life. As a franchisee, whether you manage three people or thirty-three people, it's important that you treat every one of them, not just as your subordinates or employees, but also as individuals. I feel this is an important issue and I will expand upon it later.

In terms of "feedback," it's important that you always take the position that everyone has something to contribute. The business world is replete with stories where someone who worked in the mailroom came up with an idea that saved hundreds or thousands of dollars. It goes to say that anyone in the organization can make a contribution and it's important that they be provided a forum for offering their feedback, whether it's done unilaterally or as a result of encouraging them to contribute. In some cases, it may require a bit more effort; however, don't ever feel that because someone doesn't speak up, they don't have something to say.

"Understanding" means knowing the job that needs to be done. I think every leader has to have a good understanding of what it takes to do the job and do it right. Obviously, that doesn't mean that one must be a technocrat or financial wizard needing to know every single thing that is going on in their company. However, I think it is important to have a fundamental grasp on what makes a successful business operation, whether it's fast food, temporary employment, home services, remodeling or health and fitness programs. Every individual who leads a business has to have some understanding as to what the formula for success is for that particular business.

"Accountability" refers to the fact that people must have responsibility and accountability for the job that they are charged to perform and that they receive the results of their performance. Too often, I have seen people in business that have not done a good job, not being told that their performance was below standards. I believe that everyone is entitled to know how well he or she is doing his or her job. If the job results are not up to standards they should be told, so that they can be in the position to improve their performance accordingly. Employees have to know what they are expected to do and the leader and motivator must make sure that someone is verifying that they are doing the job that they are paid to perform.

The next area that I want to discuss is recognition. "Recognition" is something that everyone seeks. There have been numerous employee satisfaction studies over the years that show that salary is not rated the number-one motivator for the majority of people. Working conditions and recognition for a job well done are very important in the hierarchy of needs. The point is people want to be recognized. They want to be recognized for a job well done; they want to be recognized for their contribution and for doing what they are being paid to do.

I indicated earlier that there are certain negative factors to leadership and motivation, and I want to compare these to the positive factors that I just presented. If you have any business experience at all, you should certainly consider these factors and you probably have had some experience from a personal standpoint in particular situations. I bring these up because as a franchisee and business owner, you need to demonstrate proper leadership and motivational practices.

Don't fall victim to what I consider to be the three negative factors that will basically destroy the positive factors. I indicated how feedback was very important. People should be heard, but it doesn't mean that we do everything that is suggested, nor does it mean that every comment or suggestion someone has is appropriate. Nevertheless, I think people should have an opportunity to be heard. Whether it's through a formal appraisal process, suggestion box, or other forum, people are entitled to be able to provide their feedback.

The negative factor to feedback is ego. By this, I mean the leader or manager who feels that no one really knows more than they do, that they truly know what is best for the organization, franchise or their company. It does not mean that the leader diminishes his authority in any way by sacrificing a bit of ego to hear what someone has to say, but rather that the opportunity be available.

Throughout my experience in franchising and business, I have seen many instances where a franchisee or a group of franchisees might have a suggestion and it's not heard because of that certain three-letter word, "ego." In some cases, the president, CEO, or someone else in a position of authority feels that they know better and no one else will tell them how a job or function can be performed more efficiently. I am not getting involved in psychology, but in its simplest form, I am sure you can think about or relate to a situation where perhaps someone didn't listen to you or didn't entertain a suggestion that you felt was positive because of "ego." As a business owner, be sure that you don't fall into that trap and destroy the creativity and enthusiasm of your employees by discouraging feedback.

I discussed respect, and how important it is to respect individuals and treat them a certain way. You want them to feel that the job they are doing is important which is how you build an effective team. You can use any analogy you want for winning, whether it's in professional sports or the business world and probably 99.9 percent of the time when you have a high level of success and achievement, you will find that people are treated with respect, especially in today's day and age. This is not the 1920s or 1930s and the philosophy that management is always right. If you want to achieve that, you need to utilize respect. The negative factor of respect is arrogance. By arrogance, I mean a certain attitude or philosophy that the leader portrays and presents to his employees, whether it's a small franchise of five employees or a large franchise operation of fifty employees. It's when the leader conducts himself or herself in a manner that portrays themselves better than the rest of the members of the organization. You know that old adage, "A chain is only as strong as its weakest link." There is a reason sayings like that have endured over the years. It's because they make so much sense and if you think about successful businesses leaders, you will always read about how their employees were treated with respect. This does not mean and it does not say that an employee cannot be fired or disciplined. If someone doesn't do their job they should be dealt with accordingly. What it does mean is that they are entitled to a level of respect. An arrogant attitude on the part of the leader or other members of the management team will destroy that important positive factor of leadership and motivation.

I am sure each of you can recall how important recognition was to you, whether as a small child or as a member of an athletic team or a club in school. All of us want recognition and it's a trait that humans share. The negative factor or the offset to recognition is indifference. Indifference is when an employee has been working for someone and has done a good job, but they are not considered for a salary increase or bonus or other way of recognizing their contribution and performance. Believe me, throughout my long business career, I have seen numerous supervisors operate small businesses whose philosophy was "unless someone asks for the raise, I don't bother. Don't volunteer it. Keep everything quiet and if someone wants something, then you can give it to them." Of course, when that same employee leaves to work for a competitor that same supervisor can't understand why and blames the employee. That trait of indifference, that attitude, will diminish your ability to be able to lead and motivate your staff.

In this chapter, I've included what I consider to represent the important principles that one should follow in order to be an effective leader and motivator. Whether you are a franchisee with four employees or whether you have four hundred, consider the traits that I presented in terms of not only your employees, but also the customers that utilize your products or services.

Is there any doubt in your mind that your customers wouldn't want respect or given the opportunity to provide feedback? Whether it's "I hope you're all set" or "do you need anything else." I am sure all customers like to be asked for their comments. Obviously, they like to be recognized. Recognition for a customer is far different than it may be for an employee. Nevertheless, it's the same principle, the same trait that's important. Whether you are dealing with your customers, your clients or your employees, these traits are very important.

How many times have you been in that favorite restaurant that you truly enjoy when the owner or waiter came up to you just to make sure that everything is fine? This is something that I know you remember, and it is probably the reason that you keep going back. From my own personal experience, I can certainly say that it's a motivating factor for me to want to be recognized and also appreciated for the business that I am providing to that particular restaurant. The same principles that should guide you in leading and motivating your employees are the same principles that your customers come to expect. It's just common sense, whether it's your customers or whether it's you as a customer, you seek to be recognized, appreciated and whether you need to or not, the opportunity to be able to provide your feedback. Don't be mistaken, however, and attribute these positive factors of leadership and motivation to only yourself. If you have a large organization or rely upon a particular supervisor in your franchise, you want to be sure that they exercise those same traits.

Most franchisees operate small businesses and for that reason many of your employees may have worked in a small business environment, and are not familiar with the same kind of atmosphere that one finds in a large company. For any of us that have worked in large companies, we certainly have realized that activities, processes, and procedures are highly organized. There is a routine schedule for time off, for giving raises, and performance evaluations. The large companies generally have everything considered, but when you enter the small business world things are usually a little different because you are working within a company that does not have hundreds of employees. It's important that you have similar guidelines for your business so that your employees feel that everyone is treated fairly.

I can recall a franchise owner who acquired a franchise in the Midwest. The franchisor I had been working with had a motto for all of our franchisees, namely, "You need to be hands-on," which meant that the franchisee needed to be directly involved in the business. It was a business that required the franchisee to be out in the public making sales calls and being actively involved with potential clients. Well, this one particular franchisee that had worked for a large company came in and immediately conducted his affairs as if he were the general manager of General Motors. So, despite all of his know-how, intelligence, experience, and quite frankly, financial success in the corporate world, he had a difficult time adjusting to a small business environment. After a number of sessions with the franchisee, I finally encouraged and convinced him that he needed to be outside his office and making personal sales calls. Being a small business owner he couldn't afford not to be a very highly productive member of his franchise operation. So, whatever franchise business you acquire, always keep that fact in mind, namely, that in most franchise operations, the franchise owner has to be a very productive member of the team and cannot simply sit in the back office shouting orders. I know this may sound like a rather elementary statement to make, but nevertheless, you would be surprised how many people get involved in a franchise and end up not doing what they need to do to be successful.

Let me recap what I consider to be the positive factors of leadership and motivation and which hopefully, can lead you to be successful:

> Your ability and knowledge of understanding the job that has to be done.
> Respect for your employees.
> Feedback from your employees.
> Accountability from your employees. They have to know what's expected of them and they have to be told when they are not doing the job.
> Recognition on behalf of your employees.

Once again, these qualities of leadership and motivation do not reside among only the top earners, but can exist throughout an organization from the largest to the smallest. I am sure that during your life you have encountered individuals whom you have admired, whether it's a schoolteacher, a football coach, a professor or your parents. Whoever it was, I would be very surprised if these individuals did not possess these same traits and qualities, which is why you remember these people.

Consider that as a business owner, people look to you for leadership and they look to you for motivation. They look to you to help give them confidence and comfort in knowing that they are doing the right job. I can assure you that if you follow the principles that I just espoused, you should be just fine in leading and motivating your employees.

CHAPTER 8

The Franchisee Commandments

Franchisees have more power than they think.

After having worked for over twenty-five years in franchising with several different companies, I have personally observed over one thousand franchise operations in various stages of growth from start-ups to ultimately being sold. I've also been involved with numerous franchisees that have faced challenges, both personal and financial and have provided operational and financial solutions to numerous franchisees that have looked for a remedy to their problems.

Based upon this experience I have developed the Franchisee Commandments. These Franchisee Commandments are based upon my own experience in franchising. I feel that these Franchisee Commandments are credible and will provide you the opportunity to benefit from them.

THE FRANCHISEE COMMANDMENTS

1. Franchisees Have More Power than They Think.

I have seen numerous franchisees with the attitude that they don't have the authority to speak up. They feel that the franchisor has them "under their thumb." Obviously, there are franchisees that are an exception, especially those who have multiple locations or are financially strong. I speak more to the typical franchisee, the single-unit owner/operator who may feel that if he/she complains too loud that the franchisor may exert some punitive control over them. I would say that this could not be further from the truth. In fact, I believe that those franchisees that provide positive and reasonable criticism to the franchisor are usually well received, particularly if it is from franchisees that have been following the franchisor program. This doesn't mean that every franchisor will accept criticism with open arms, but I have found that most franchisors are willing to accept feedback and suggestions from their franchisees. For that reason, I would hope that as a franchisee, you recognize that you have more power than you think and that you speak up when necessary.

2. Franchisees Should Always Relate to Successful Franchisees.

I don't know how many times I have seen franchisees listen to the so-called critics of the franchisor. Those franchisees that have not achieved any significant success themselves and seem to spend most of their time looking for excuses for their poor performance. I have always told my franchisees, "If you want to learn about how to be successful then listen to the successful franchisees. Don't listen to the chronic complainers."

My strategy whenever I got involved in a franchise system where there was work to be done was to establish the successful franchisees as the reference point for the other franchisees. I remember my very first assignment as a regional director. I had twenty-one franchisees in the retail food business. There were several franchisees that were constantly criticizing the system and practices of the franchisor. Sometimes I thought they got tremendous joy just hearing themselves speak. It was interesting to note that those same franchisees were the ones who were also the least successful in my region and their performance could be truthfully stated as "mediocre." Fortunately for me, they represented a minority of the franchisees, so my first goal at meetings and in my regional newsletters was to reference the successful franchisees wherever possible. I did this on a regular basis, and after no more than six or seven months, the franchisees started to relate to the more successful ones and were turned off by those who were the constant complainers.

3. **Franchisees Need to Document Violations of Their Franchise Agreement.**

I can't emphasize this strongly enough. As a franchisee, if you encounter certain problems and issues with the franchisor or with an employee of the franchisor, such as a field representative, make sure that you document those situations. Even if you don't send a letter or an e-mail to the franchisor representative, be sure that you make note of the time, date, and occurrence of an event. This is very important because one never knows when there may be a problem in the future. Having spent my career as a franchisor as well as a franchisee for a period of time, I can tell you that any franchisor "worth their salt" will "document." Clearly, the franchisee should do the same.

I have been involved in numerous depositions where the franchisee had claims denied because they had no corroborating evidence. They were not able to document many of the claims that they made because so much of what they did was verbal, and as such they could not even recite the correct dates, time, etc. I am not advocating that as a franchisee you make a journal entry every time something minor happens with the franchisor. Rather, I am suggesting that if you encounter any problems with the franchisor or with one of their representatives that has a negative impact on your business, you should document the facts. In terms of elevating the documentation to communicating with the franchisor, I think that becomes a judgment that has to be based upon each case. Its important for you to seek advice from your franchise attorney when you get to the point that you feel you should notify your franchisor of violations.

4. Franchisees Must Accept a Strong Franchise Agreement in Order to Protect the System.

This may seem like somewhat of an oxymoron for a franchisee, but I found so many times over the years that a good strong franchise agreement protects the franchisee. It protects the franchisee from those franchisees that don't follow the system and fail to do what they are required to.

As I have indicated previously in this book, can you imagine a weak noncompete provision in the franchise agreement? You could end up having some of your colleagues leaving the system, opening up a competing business and competing against you down the street.

Franchisees have to accept the principle that they are part of a network. The franchisor needs to have certain devices within that agreement to protect the network for everyone. It is not a case of the franchisor necessarily protecting them; it is a case of the franchisor wanting to protect the network, which consists of the franchisees.

In terms of "quality standards" consider being in the franchise food business and some franchisees didn't follow the operating standards and had dirty outlets. That will directly impact the trade name you are depending upon. It would affect your own franchise if this noncompliant franchisee were in your geographic area.

5. Franchisees Have a Vested Interest in the Financial Viability of the Franchisor.

I have found that most franchisees recognize that their success, opportunity for future growth, profits and return from the sale of their franchise will be a direct result of having a strong, financially viable franchisor. Many years ago, one of the franchisors I worked with faced a situation where profits had decreased due to an overall sales decline. The CEO of that franchisor made a plea to the franchisees to conduct some aggressive marketing. The reason was so that the franchisor could become more profitable and turn their financial situation around. If you think about it, it would not be unusual to have a network of franchisees that are successful yet have a franchisor that is not profitable. This CEO made an important comment. He said in order to compete and be successful you need to be financially strong. In order for the franchise system to be strong, viable, and competitive, you need to have a financially viable franchisor.

Someone once said, "The franchisees should be given exactly what they are entitled to and the franchisor should receive what it's entitled to, no more or no less. However, there may be a point in time when franchisees may be required to 'cooperate' with their franchisor for the best interests of the entire system."

6. The Most Successful Franchisees Are Those Who Follow the Program.

I can't tell you how many different franchise systems I've worked in where the franchisees that were the most profitable and successful were the ones who "followed the program." Now, I am not necessarily speaking about just a turnkey operation but I am speaking about operations that were a product or format franchise, where the franchisees sold a product manufactured by the franchisor or other products or services. In both cases, those franchisees who followed the system and the general program as prescribed by the franchisor were the most profitable. I don't think I can recall one franchisee that I would characterize as somewhat rebellious or who did their own thing as having had a profitable operation. To the contrary, usually those who failed to follow the program were the ones who had the problems. This does not mean that every franchisor has a secret formula for success. It is a given that over the course of the year, they will always be some franchisees who unfortunately will fail.

Obviously, there are certain systems that are highly sophisticated and so highly organized that most franchisees can truly succeed if they do what they are required to. On the other hand, there are a number of franchisees that own franchises that require more independent decision making and action on the part of the franchisee. In those cases, I would suggest that those franchisees that are most successful typically would follow the franchise program and advice of the franchisor.

7. Profitability Should Proceed Franchisee Expansion.

I have observed so many examples, during my career, of franchisees having an unquenchable thirst for territory. They are always looking for another option, planning ahead to open up another store, location or office before they are profitable with their existing location. You may be reading this thinking, I will never do that; however what happens is that a franchisee opens the business, may be marginally profitable and starts thinking, "If I only had another location or a little more territory, I could grow this business to be much larger." They will then approach the franchisor, which in most cases is looking to sell more territory. The franchisor often agrees to give the franchisee more territory, and the franchisee does, in fact, acquire it with plans to expand.

If the franchisee does not have a strong, viable, and profitable operation preceding this expansion, the chances are that franchisee is going to have problems. The reason for this is that it's going to require capital to develop an additional location and its territory. Capital is generated by a positive cash flow, which stems from a profitable operation. If you don't have that, then surely you are going to find yourself in a difficult position.

My experience has been that franchisees that maximize their existing territory are the ones who will typically end up being the most profitable and create the greatest amount of wealth for themselves and their operation. When they do expand they are in a much better position to do so.

8. Franchisee Unity Is Power.

If franchisees have some issues, the best way to resolve those issues is to seek input as well as advice from their fellow franchisees. It goes without saying that franchisees have a strong need to protect their business and investment. Therefore, it is not out of the ordinary to expect that franchisees will be concerned about their own individual situation. I have had experience with franchisees calling me up and telling me that certain franchisees call them up to complain. The response by the franchisee is "I have all I can do to run my business and I don't want to get involved in that." This goes back to one of my previous comments about the more successful franchisees. They are not usually the critics because they are too busy running their business and being a success. Yet when they do speak they are usually heard.

However, there may be times when franchisees do have major issues and are not heard. In these situations, there is absolutely no doubt that a unified group of franchisees can be extremely powerful and capable of eliciting a response from the franchisor. I don't think there are many franchisors that would not be responsive to a unified group of franchisees. I have witnessed a group of franchisees representing the bulk of the revenue in their system sign a letter listing their concerns and then sending the letter to the franchisor. If you don't think that wasn't well received, you are highly mistaken, because a meeting was scheduled by the franchisor, probably within twenty-four hours after receiving the letter. It's common sense and it goes without saying that no franchisor wants to face the possibility of having influential members of their network up in arms over problems. It may simply mean that the franchisees want to be heard and are just looking for some answers to their questions. If you are part of a franchise system that has a franchise advisory council which meets on a regular basis, there may already be a vehicle in place where you can speak with a unified voice.

9. Franchisees Must Always Select the Most Accomplished, Articulate, and Reasonable Franchisees for the Franchise Advisory Council

I have been responsible for establishing a number of Franchise Advisory Councils and have been in situations where the franchisee's selected their representatives and where the franchisor chose the representatives.

I'll explain the reason for the difference. In one company where I set up a Franchise Advisory Council, I needed to get it established rather quickly, I selected four (4) representatives for the Franchise Advisory Council—one from each geographic area. I didn't select franchisees that were profranchisor, so to speak, but I selected those whom I considered to be successful franchisees that also would be willing to speak up. I purposely avoided those who were considered the "troublemakers" or those who were not very successful. After the first meeting or two, the franchisees voted on the representatives. They voted on representatives whom they thought would truly represent their best interests.

In another situation, I can remember starting up a Franchise Advisory Council where there was a vote which included six (6) regions in the country, and sure enough, there was a campaign by several franchisees to be on the committee; a number of the better performing franchisees were not interested. The franchisees ended up electing six (6) franchise advisory members of which four (4) were the more outspoken and rebellious franchisees out of about eighty (80) that we had in the network. The result was that when we had our first meeting, we ended up having to sit there and listen to these franchisees whining and complaining about their own personal situations, rather than focusing on the concerns of their constituents. For that reason, I think it is important if you are in a situation where there is a Franchise Advisory Council, to make sure you look toward those franchisees to represent you who have been successful, articulate, and reasonable.

10. The Franchisee Should Use an Experienced Franchisee Attorney.

If you find yourself in a situation where a dispute or disagreement with the franchisor escalates to the point that you require legal representation, be sure you have strong legal counsel. There is no doubt that having an experienced franchise attorney will be in your overall best interest. Franchising is still somewhat of a specialized legal practice and there is a knowledge base and experience level that good franchise attorneys will have. By not hiring an effective franchise attorney to represent you, there is a risk of having an attorney who has not faced a situation in franchising similar to yours. You may believe that you are saving a few dollars in the beginning but you could pay more in the end.

These are my "Franchisee Commandments." I feel that they can serve as a guideline for you as you operate as a franchisee within your network. These Franchisee Commandments are not foolproof and it doesn't mean that there are not exceptions, but I think generally, these will run true to form in most cases. It's probably a good idea to keep these in your mind as you conduct your affairs as a franchisee and be guided accordingly.

CHAPTER 9

Franchisee/Franchisor Relations

The spirit of the relationship must exist in an
environment of mutual trust and respect.

If there is one subject that I feel eminently qualified to discuss, it's franchisee/franchisor relations. By virtue of having spent most of my career in the area of operations, I was often placed in the position of being directly involved in litigation, brought by either the franchisee or the franchisor.

I have also had the responsibility for resolving or mediating disputes between the franchisee and franchisor. In fact, in one company where I worked, I was known affectionately as the "secretary of state" because if there was an issue with a particular franchisee, it was felt that I could speak to that individual and diplomatically defuse the situation and take those steps which would lead to a resolution of the problem.

William Dion, the owner of the ATC Medical Staffing Services franchise in Charleston, South Carolina, offers his assessment of the franchisee/franchisor relationship as follows: "The relationship between a franchisee and franchisor must be a give-give situation. Both parties must operate as partners in the endeavor. This is contrary to what is stated in most franchise agreements since there is usually wording in the agreement which states that the relationship does not constitute a partnership. This language is to denote what the exact role of the parties really is. With all that said, if both parties are not committed to the venture for the 'long haul' and are unwilling to keep investing money and energy then the franchise system will not grow and both parties will suffer."

The spirit of the relationship must exist in an environment of mutual trust and respect. However, in some cases, disputes and disagreement do arise and the objective for both franchisee and franchisor is to prevent disputes from escalating out of control. Litigation between the parties can be very costly and not just in terms of money.

As the comedian Alan King once said, "There was a judge who had a painting of a cow behind his desk. Pulling on the horns was the defendant, pulling on the tail was the plaintiff, and underneath, milking the cow were the attorneys." This, I promise you, is my first and last attorney joke. In fact, I can truthfully say that some of my best friends are attorneys.

The important point is that litigation is very expensive. It's expensive in terms of time, money, and relationships. I have been involved in some very rare situations where there was litigation, the issue was resolved and the franchisee stayed in the system and continued to have a very positive and productive relationship with the franchisor. In fact, that particular franchisee continued to be a very good validator if a prospective franchisee called regarding the franchise opportunity. This outcome is the exception and does not happen in many cases; in some instances, animosity usually remains between the parties.

As a new franchisee, it's important that you are aware of ways to avoid acrimonious disputes with the franchisor. The majority of franchisees working within a franchise organization are productive and rarely have a major issue with the franchisor. Do they have certain issues? Of course. As I said at the very beginning of this book, there is no such thing as the perfect franchise and whenever you are dealing with individuals, there will always be some problems that will arise. Hopefully, these problems will be minor and can be easily resolved.

I indicated earlier in this book that most franchisees fail to recognize the clout that they have and that some are reluctant to complain to the franchisor. Here is an example of how well I know this to be true. At an early point in my career, I recall telling one of my bosses about some complaints that some of our franchisees had, only to have it fall on deaf ears without any action taken. Yet, sometime later when the same message was delivered by a franchisee, there was an immediate response to the situation. It's a fact that franchisees speak with much more authority than most of them realize. Be forewarned, however, you need credibility and you can't be a franchisee who doesn't follow the program and/or is a poor performer and expect to be heard. If you are in this category, you might be heard, but there may not be any follow through.

Typically, franchisors will listen and pay heed to feedback from their franchisees. In fact, the higher you go in the franchisor organization, the more likely you'll be heard and taken seriously. If someone at the top of the organization does not hear you, then you didn't follow my advice when you evaluated the franchisor, or there has been a dramatic change in the organization. So, don't be afraid to speak up when you feel that you need to.

I recall a franchisee that had been with the franchisor a long time. It was the first franchise company that I worked for. This franchisee told me that as far as he was concerned, he always wanted to work in an environment where the franchise agreement was put in his desk drawer and the only time it was taken out would be to see when it expired. Of course, that's probably the ultimate in positive franchise relations, but nevertheless, that's how that particular franchisee saw his role within that franchise company. He would always prefer to try to talk through a problem rather than to send the franchisor a nasty letter. The fact that the founders of the company were always willing to listen to their franchisees and respond to their concerns certainly fostered a positive environment. When it comes to franchise litigation, it's been my experience that when a franchisee sues a franchisor, there are, at minimum, three main issues:

1. The franchisee was misled or promised certain items that the franchisor never delivered;
2. The franchisee never received all of the training and assistance they needed; and
3. If a franchisee had some problems, they never received help or assistance from the franchisor.

I recall only one lawsuit where the franchisee did not include these three (3) items in the complaint. It was so obvious that I told my colleagues about this unique occurrence.

I would suggest the best way to avoid getting involved in any kind of an issue that could escalate into a major problem with the franchisor is to make sure you follow three key steps right at the beginning. Although, I can't guarantee that following these steps will always work, you can be sure that if you do have a battle with the franchisor you'll have excellent documentation to support your position.

1. If you have a problem or issue, you need to make sure that you communicate that to the franchisor representative as soon as possible. This may be a field supervisor, or it could be the contact that you have at corporate headquarters, whoever that individual is. I would consider a problem to be something fairly significant, not when something arrived an hour late, but something that can impact your business or your profits, etc.; make sure you communicate that.
2. Make absolutely sure that you document that event. Don't rely on a phone call. I have seen many examples where a franchisee in litigation would say, "Well, I called and I reported

it eight times," and then during a deposition, when asked did they have documentation regarding this matter, they would say no. Obviously, it doesn't prove anything unless you have documentation. So, my second point is that you must make sure you document your issue or complaint and whom you sent that to. I am a big believer in e-mail because I think that e-mail does two things. It takes away all of the hiding places and it creates a documentation trail. Someone can't say they didn't get the fax or the letter didn't arrive. With e-mail you have a clear trail that can be documented. In any case, send a simple note or e-mail and don't threaten.

3. Make sure that you receive a response to the problem or issue that you have. If you don't, then follow up until you do. If you don't receive a response after a second or third request, then I would suggest that you "go up the ladder." If the problem is of a major consequence, go to the CEO or president level.

I recall a situation when I was working with a certain franchisor. We were the prime tenants on the location leases and we sublet to the franchisee. Since some leases were rather old, their value had significantly increased, yet the rent paid by the franchisees remained far below market value. As the subleases were about to expire, we would propose an increase in the rent so as to be comparable to market rates.

Some franchisees objected to this change and called the company's real estate director. When this person was criticized for making this policy change, he claimed it wasn't his decision. After further questioning, he stated that the "Finance Committee" made this decision. When the franchisees asked who were on this committee, the real estate director told them he couldn't disclose the names.

Of course, to the franchisees who had pressed the issue, they found themselves up against a secret committee who met in the dark of night. The end result was that the real estate director lost all credibility because he was unwilling to "take the heat." The franchisees ultimately met with the president of the company who gave them a chance to vent but, nevertheless, did not alter the new sublease policy.

Most franchisors will recognize franchisees that act professionally and who document their problems and suggestions. Franchisors will be a lot more responsive to e-mail or a letter than a simple telephone call. Obviously, this is not true for all franchisors and it doesn't mean that this is right. It doesn't mean that someone shouldn't respond just as readily to a verbal concern or complaint as to one in writing, but the difference is that some franchisors may tend to think in terms of potential litigation and look at what could be damaging in the future. Anything that is documented definitely provides a benefit to the individual who has a grievance. I have been involved in litigation where I have been deposed and have testified in court. Additionally, I consider myself, although not an attorney, very knowledgeable when it comes to franchise dispute resolution and litigation. I have gained the experience to recognize when there is going to be a problem, and because of that, I have been able to resolve many of the issues.

Craig Tractenberg, a noted franchise attorney with Nixon Peabody, LLC, states, "Franchisees need to strive for candor in their relationship with the franchisor." Tractenberg feels that the franchisee ought to comply with the system, yet communicate constructive changes to the franchisor. "If there is a better way to perform a task or operate the franchise, the franchisee should make every effort to bring this information to the attention of their franchisor."

I have seen my share of franchisees who didn't do what they were advised to do. We have all heard about franchisees having issues and problems. Now let me clear the air so to speak and make it abundantly clear that it's not just the franchisor that may have been the cause of the problem. I can assure you that I have seen my share of franchisees that were responsible for the problem. Some of these same franchisees, after having a problem, tried to blame the franchisor. It is not always a case of the franchisor not doing what they should be doing. Sometimes the franchisee is not performing and not fulfilling their obligations under the franchise agreement, which may cause them problems.

If the franchisee does have a perceived issue or problem and they document and communicate that to the franchisor, then the odds are exceedingly high that they will get a response, most probably in writing from the franchisor who hopefully will help to resolve that problem or issue. In some cases, I have seen problems that were raised by franchisees to be a simple misunderstanding, whereby they interpreted something in the agreement a certain way that wasn't true. It might have been something that they misunderstood in terms of what was said to them when they first acquired the franchise, which is why franchise agreements have a provision, which in layman's terms says, "If it isn't in this agreement, it doesn't exist." So, I would be totally dishonest if I didn't say that problems might come from both sides of the relationship; however, if an issue is carefully documented, then usually it will receive the right response.

Neither the franchisee nor the franchisor enters a franchise relationship with the intent of failing. It goes without saying that both parties want to be successful. The franchisor wants franchisees to succeed and they may suggest various ways to the franchisee as the best way to achieve success. I remember asking franchisees the question, "You've really been successful, what is your secret?" and they said, "I have followed the program." In other words, they followed the advice of the franchisor.

There is no doubt that the most dangerous franchisee in my experience is the entrepreneur who wants to be a franchisee, but is unwilling to give up their freedom. You just cannot have both. You can't be a true entrepreneur and be part of a franchise system. This is just the way it is. The franchisor must have a certain degree of control over their network for many reasons, some of which I mentioned in prior chapters. So for this reason, if you happen to fall into that category and you have been in the program for a few months and you like to do different things and experiment, you will find out that you will become a square peg in a round hole. Just maybe you should cut your losses and speak to the franchisor about a way to exit the system. I will devote some time to that issue later on, but it goes without saying that if you have any issues with the franchisor, get them out on the table and try to resolve them. Follow my three recommendations: communicate, document, and make sure that you receive a response.

I would also suggest that you gain a snapshot of the franchise system regarding problem or dispute resolution. Speak to some of the franchisees that have been with the program for a certain number of years and ask them if they had any issues, and if so, how have they been resolved. This is obviously predicated on the fact that you are a part of a more mature franchise organization and that they have a number of franchisees that have been involved with that organization for a certain number of years. You should recall this as one of the questions you were to ask existing franchisees when you begin your franchising process.

If, on the other hand, you happen to be part of a new franchise company that is not at the mature growth stage whereby there is a limited number of franchisees, then I think it is incumbent upon you to maintain an ongoing dialogue with existing franchisees for the following reasons:

1. Because you are with a small franchisor that is growing, there is no real track record.
2. There may not be a high level of experience on the part of the franchisor in dealing with problems or issues.
3. The franchisor may not have the organizational structure or resources to be able to address some of the issues that arise.

For these reasons, if you happen to be part of a small franchise company, it is incumbent upon you to maintain a dialogue with several franchisees on a regular basis so that you are able to share information regarding certain issues and problems.

I also recommend that you have a relationship with one or two franchisees that includes a get-together for lunch or dinner or, at the very least, a regular dialogue even if it's on the telephone every few weeks. Everyone is busy trying to run their business and grow sales, but surely you can find the time during the course of the week or month to exchange information with one another. I am not suggesting that you have some structured organization, but simply that there is an exchange of information and an ongoing dialogue so that you are aware of what is happening within your franchise company.

Franchise Advisory Councils are a necessary ingredient of any successful franchise organization. I have been involved with franchisors where there was no Franchise Advisory Council, and I was involved in one organization that had what was referred to by some members of the franchisor staff as a vigilante group, not unlike the backroom meetings of the Wild West many years ago. Basically, this was a group of franchisees that were upset with the advertising program that was structured by the franchisor. The issue was resolved when certain franchisees participated in an advertising committee formed by the franchisor, which was the resolution to the problem. What this revealed was that when franchisees feel that they don't have a voice or are not heard, they will seek comfort and affiliation with one another so that they have a way of being able to gain attention and control over the franchisor.

The important point to keep in mind is that if you do encounter a problem with a franchisor be reasonable and make sure that you don't come across as antagonistic. During my career, those franchisees that appear to be always causing a problem were the ones who were watched very closely, since we were concerned that we would end up having a confrontation with them. So, I suggest that if you have issues be reasonable and respectful and usually any problems will get worked out.

I think one of the most rewarding benefits of being a franchisee is to become a member of the International Franchise Association. My intent is not to promote the IFA for the sake of promoting them, but rather, because they offer a tremendous choice of services for franchisees whereby one can learn a great deal about franchising.

The dues for a franchisee are very reasonable. By being a member you are able to participate in IFA functions, workshops, receive literature, and have an opportunity to learn much more about franchising, from not only a franchisee perspective, but also from a franchisor perspective. Also, being a member of the IFA will afford you the opportunity to participate at various functions and interface and interact with other franchisees. This can be a very rewarding experience in terms of your gaining more knowledge about franchising and understanding more about relationship building, dispute resolution, and hopefully to becoming more successful. There are other organizations such as the American Association of Franchisees and Dealers that offer advice and guidance to primarily prospective and existing franchisees.

Resolving disputes and having a positive and viable relationship with the franchisor is an important element for success. It's been my personal experience, as well as practice, to respond favorably to franchisees that have been team players. By the way, being team players does not mean that a franchisee bows down to every request of the franchisor or has nothing but good things to say about the franchisor. It basically means that the franchisee is concerned about the overall interest of not only their own business but also the franchise network in general. They recognize that a franchisee that doesn't follow the program, doesn't run a clean store, or doesn't service their clients correctly is negatively impacting not only them but also obviously the entire network and that you, as a franchisee, will suffer as well.

Positive franchisee/franchisor relations don't just happen but rather require a good deal of effort on the part of both parties. Despite the fact that you may be in a situation where the franchisor is not as responsive and cooperative as you believe they should be, don't lose faith. With the right franchisee structure and proper communication effectively applied, I've seen franchisees cause a major change on the part of the franchisor. Remember, not every franchisor has the experience and knowledge in knowing how they should react and respond to their franchisees. It's unfortunate but the truth.

CHAPTER 10

Conversion Franchising

More rapid growth and brand recognition.

I would be remiss if I didn't devote at least one chapter to conversion franchising. Conversion franchising is when an existing company, which may have as little as one or two company-owned operations or outlets, decides to embark on franchising by converting their concept or operation to a franchise format. Another aspect of conversion franchising relates to companies that have a large dealer network such as the case with Century 21, whereby they convert existing independently owned businesses to a franchise operation. Whatever route one follows, the objective is to take an existing operation and convert it to a franchise program.

For those companies that seek rapid growth combined with the security of having owner-operators, franchising provides a multitude of opportunities. During my franchise career, I have had the good fortune to administer and participate in conversions of both dealers and corporate-owned locations into franchise operations. These experiences took place with different companies.

The first conversion that I was involved with had to do with a large manufacturer—we will refer to as Company A—that was investing in a national advertising program which generated a large number of customer leads for its high-quality product line. Some of the dealers who were selling Company A's products and receiving leads from Company A were in the position of diverting customers from the advertised products to competitors products made by Company B. Despite the fact that the dealers had a sales quota requirement which had to be met in order for them to remain an authorized dealer of Company A, it was apparent that many of the dealers were simply leveraging the reputation, product line, and marketing of Company A to promote competitive products.

Our solution in securing a committed dealer network and an equitable relationship for Company A with its loyal dealers was to introduce a franchise conversion program. The conversion, which took about a year and a half to complete, resulted in a national franchise network of 150 locations. These new franchisees were required to adhere to specific operational and performance guidelines. This conversion program combined with a renewed focus on the part of Company A, now a franchisor, and its newly developed franchise network resulted in a more formidable organization.

The former dealers now owned a franchise with more value and brand recognition and they were a much more integrated part of Company A's network. Those dealers who represented a minority of the original network, and were not committed, decided not to convert and either remained as dealers or dropped out of the program entirely. The end result was a win-win situation for both parties, the company and its new franchise network.

I have also been responsible for the conversion of an acquired network of company-owned locations into a franchise operation. In one particular case, my company was able to recapture a significant portion of its acquisition costs by selling and franchising the company-owned locations it had recently acquired as part of a major acquisition. The result was a franchise network of committed owner-operators with a vested interest in their business.

The following examples demonstrate the benefits that conversion franchising can provide:

- More rapid growth and brand recognition
- Organizational and network stability
- Franchisor can operate with fewer staff versus corporate operations
- Increased purchasing power for the entire network
- Security of local ownership
- More consistent earnings flow
- Synergy from owner-operators

However, there are some drawbacks from converting, which include:

- Well-run corporate locations are more profitable for the company versus franchise operations.
- You can't fire a franchisee, plus more overall control over corporate locations.
- Legal costs of franchising can be high.
- Organizational staff will require some changes to adapt to franchise operations.

If you have an interest in converting your operations into a franchise, there are several questions that need to be answered before you proceed in investing the necessary capital and people resources:

The Franchise Business

The business that will operate as a franchise must have certain unique attributes that will appeal to prospective franchisees. There must be certain characteristics of your business that are not readily duplicated and will allow for marketing the products or services as well as to market the franchise opportunity. If the business concept of the franchise is lacking, then there will be barriers to success.

Ability to Package the System

There must be the capability to duplicate the successful elements of the operation. A key benefit of franchising is the ability of the franchisee to acquire a business with processes or practices which, when followed by the franchisee, will typically lead to success. Note, I say typically because there is no guarantee that the franchisees will be successful; however, the risk of failure should be far less with the franchise operation.

Regardless of whether the product is food or services, the business, which is being converted to a franchise, must have the capability of being set into a system.

The difference between a Century 21 conversion program versus a more traditional conversion of existing corporate offices is that Century 21 utilized a concentrated marketing effort to attract a large network of independent real estate brokers. Under this approach the independent brokers could become part of a large network, which could capture a greater share of the residential real estate market.

It's important not to confuse this type of conversion franchising with converting an existing business to a franchise, which I discuss in the next chapter. For example, if you happen to own two outlets that sell a line of food products and you desire to franchise this operation you should follow the test that I am outlining in this chapter; however, this form of franchising is far different than someone who takes and combines a large fragmented network of independent operators into one program under one specific brand name. In addition to Century 21, Mr. Build, which was based upon combining a group of independent individuals in the buildings trade such as roofers, plumbers, painters, etc., is another example where a conversion franchise was based upon consolidating independent companies into a franchise utilizing a common trade name and strong marketing to market the products and services.

At this point, I would like to relate a rather humorous episode in my career that involved conversion franchising. While working with a company that was in the process of converting corporate offices to franchise by selling corporate locations and simultaneously franchising it to individuals, the company also would acquire independently owned businesses and then convert those to a franchise. I can remember a discussion I had with the CFO where I referred to a company office being franchised as a conversion. He interrupted me to say, "That's really a transformation." He then said, "A conversion is when an acquired company is converted to a franchise." My response to him was, "This is beginning to sound like some kind of religious experience and I would be reluctant to start using the terms transformation and conversion when discussing the status of various company operations." I could never quite figure out the need for such a distinction; nevertheless, I continued to humor the CFO with his definitions of conversion franchising.

Successful Financial Model

The financial model must benefit both franchisor and its franchisees. Any franchise program, which unfavorably provides one party a significant financial advantage over the other, is usually doomed for failure. The model that is developed cannot result in the franchisees being more profitable on a comparable basis than the franchisor and vice versa. The best way to assure that this will not happen is to have a pilot or prototype operation, which would operate exactly like a franchise. This operation could either be an existing corporately owned location or it could be a new location that is opened up and operated just like a franchise.

Required Capital for Implementation and Growth

A new franchisor will need working capital to meet the legal expenses and staffing requirements to commence a franchise program. No one should get into franchising with the intent that they will simply convert three locations to a franchise and then not have requirements beyond that point. It's very important that you set certain requirements in terms of legal costs and organizational staff that may be required, such as franchise sales staff and supervisory or field employees, advertising to solicit franchise prospects, etc. You will also need to be prepared for the fact that as you open franchise locations there will be a time line before they will be generating financial revenue or income to you as the new franchisor.

Commitment to Franchising

There must be a true commitment to franchising as a business format for your company. During my career, I have witnessed a number of companies embark on a franchise program without being fully committed. The result was that the new franchisor failed to recognize some of the obstacles and differences that franchising brought to their organization. In some cases, it left the CEO frustrated and disillusioned about franchising. It's extremely important that the proper time and effort be invested in analyzing the advantages and disadvantages of converting your company to a franchise operation. Whether you have one location or twenty, you need to have good expert advice so that you make the right decision.

There are significant advantages to franchising, but there are also some disadvantages and it's very critical that you balance all of the various elements involved in franchising so that you go into this change appropriately.

Some people embark on a franchising program and, after the first year or so, get frustrated as a result of the fact that they can't control their franchisees like they can a corporate employee. This goes back to my comment regarding a commitment to franchising. There must be an organizational, financial, and a true philosophical commitment to franchising for it to be successful. This, of course, is assuming that the product and services that are being provided by your outlets will conform to a franchising concept.

Once you have carefully considered the various advantages and disadvantages that franchising can provide to your organization you should then make an intelligent decision whether or not you should proceed. If the answer is yes, you need to have the resources to embark upon this new venture.

Regardless of whether you choose to engage consultants, attorneys, or other professionals, it's very important that you seek competent advice before, during, and after you convert to franchising.

CHAPTER 11

Starting a Franchise

Have the required capital and get good advice.

As the franchise industry continues to grow and becomes a more attractive method of doing business, more and more individuals and small business owners view franchising as an effective way to grow.

The majority of this group consists of small companies, which may have only one location. Some may not have a single location. In any case, there continues to be a great deal of appeal that franchising offers the small business owner.

For those individuals or small business owners who have an interest in franchising their company, I have a number of suggestions that I present in this chapter. Compared to conversion franchising, which involves the conversion of independent businesses to a franchise, a new franchise start-up takes a far different route.

Starting up a new franchise program typically follows a specific path: A small business owner operating one to two locations has achieved a certain level of success in their market. Seeing this success as a possible platform to expansion, franchising becomes the logical route to follow.

There are usually two primary reasons for this decision. First, the business owner truly believes that they have developed a unique and attractive business, which lends itself to franchising; second, they do not have the capital necessary to expand their business via corporate-owned locations. The franchise model is an indirect source of capital since franchisees make an investment in their franchise operation.

There are large companies and well-capitalized individuals who engage in start-up franchises; however, in terms of total participants they don't represent the majority.

For those who are considering a start-up franchise, I would suggest that you carefully review the information in this chapter. There is a great deal of work involved in starting up a franchise program. I've put together some highlights and key points regarding this process.

1. Have the required capital to get started. The basic costs for developing a "bare bones" franchise can range from $75,000 to $100,000. This would include the legal fees associated with constructing the UFOC (to include the franchise agreement) and filing various state registrations. Also included are feasibility studies, franchise manuals, consulting advice, strategic planning, development of marketing materials, and franchise sales. This does not include any new franchise staff, advertising for franchisee prospects, and other ancillary items. When you add this up, it could easily come to $125-$150,000 before a single franchise is sold. Obviously, it could be done for a bit less; however, there are few costs that can be reduced.

    Unless prospective franchisors have the appropriate level of capitalization, they will find it difficult to successfully start a franchise. I have had numerous inquiries from prospective clients who are surprised when told the costs of starting a franchise. The simple truth is that before you begin be sure that you have the ability to meet the minimum capital requirements.

2. Get good advice. If you have the capital necessary to launch a franchise start-up, the next step is to engage the services of a franchise expert who can evaluate your business and guide you toward your decision. You can take several routes to obtain this advice. One is to engage the services of a competent franchise consultant or use a franchise attorney. My suggestion is to first engage the services of a qualified franchise consultant so that you don't put the proverbial "cart before the horse." Before you start to consider a franchise agreement, you need to verify that your business can be successfully franchised. This will require someone who is familiar with franchising has done start-ups and has a proven track record in the franchise industry. You can locate these people on the Internet and by visiting the IFA Web site, which lists members of its Supplier Forum. When you do identify candidates, be sure to do the following:

Ask if they will do a preliminary review of your business operation being franchised and the cost. A skilled and experienced franchise consultant can perform this service in about two to three days. If you're told they only do a package of services, this might not be the right one for you. Be advised, some consulting firms may not wish to perform an initial review, which is fine. You want to be sure that before you invest a good deal of money that you're on the right course.

Be sure to ask for client references so that you can verify that the consultant has a good track record. You can also speak to one or two clients to gain some advice.

Make sure that the consultant has a mixture of industry and consulting experience. There is no better lesson than having worked in a franchise company and being exposed to all aspects of franchise operations.

You want to be sure that the expert you choose will provide the best advice possible.

Lastly, don't be "penny wise and pound foolish." If you make your decision based solely on price (within reasonable limits), then you might end up getting a lot less than you need. As my father would say, "You get what you pay for." Once you select your consultant or advisor, you can move on to the next step. You and/or your consultant can answer some of the questions in the next section.

3. Your business as a viable and attractive franchise. I haven't met many small business owners who don't have a great deal of pride regarding their business and what they have achieved. Although this pride and confidence is laudable, it can also impair the ability of the owner to evaluate their business objectively when considering franchising. Since small business owners typically exert a high degree of control over their day-to-day business operations, it's important for them to recognize that this situation won't exist under a franchise operation.

These two factors, pride of ownership and strong operational control, cannot be allowed to impair the results of judging whether the business lends itself to a successful franchise operation. This means that the owner needs to be very objective when making that determination. Rather than make a "seat of the pants" decision regarding the feasibility of franchising the owner should obtain competent advice from a qualified franchise expert. The cost of this analysis can be reasonable and could save a great deal of money if it was decided to proceed and failure follows.

Following are some preliminary questions that you can answer before franchising your business:

a. Have you registered the trademarks? You could start up and find others using your name.
b. Will the business operation and the financial results support a franchisee? The business needs to handle the expense of a royalty. It needs to be profitable.

c. Can the business operation be structured to be operated by a franchisee? The term "cookie-cutter" refers to a franchise program that is highly simplified in terms of tasks.

d. Will the operation require unique skills? If yes, it could limit potential franchisees.

e. How competitive is the business? Can it be easily duplicated or copied? You don't want to franchise and see others compete against you during your start-up stage.

f. Does the business have any market limitations? Will it be attractive in all markets or limited to certain demographics?

Once you've completed this step, then you need to move toward putting the franchise program together.

g. The Franchise Steps. If you've reached this point in the franchise process, then the next steps consist of putting the actual franchise together.

h. Your franchise attorney must put the UFOC together. This will require the insertion of the initial franchise fee and ongoing royalty. Most franchise attorneys will have a basic questionnaire, which the franchisor will complete. You will need some assistance from your consultant, financial advisor or accountant, and franchise attorney to complete this process. Before getting overly concerned, most of the information is rather basic and shouldn't require a great deal of effort.

By the way, the franchise attorney, regardless of whether you chose them or your consultant recommended them, represents you. Their job is to represent you and your company when they construct the franchise documents.

i. The operations manuals. The manuals will need to be written so as to communicate policy, procedures, and guidelines for operating the franchise. The franchise consultant based upon input and some work on your part typically does the manuals. If you already have an operating manual or written guidelines, it will make this process a bit easier.

The manuals will usually consist of an operations, marketing, and start-up or grand opening.

j. Training Program. A franchise-training program will need to be constructed. This also will be included in the UFOC. The amount and intensity of the training will depend upon the type of franchise. Training will usually follow the manuals and is most often held at franchisor's headquarters.

k. Marketing and advertising materials. You'll need to have marketing and advertising materials for your franchisees. Once printed, the franchisees can purchase it at a reasonable cost. The price should be self-liquidating. This means that as franchisor you will calculate all of the costs to produce the brochure, including design and printing. These costs are then spread over the number of brochures produced. I recommend this approach since it avoids the franchisor making a profit on supplies.

Franchise Materials. You'll need to produce franchise brochures and materials, which will be used to sell new franchises. If you don't have an existing Web site you'll need to have one built. The Web site will be used to promote your business, disclose locations, and market your franchise sales. Be sure you include your franchise attorney, so that you're not violating any franchise rules.

Staffing. Unless you intend to market your own franchises you need to consider hiring a franchise salesperson. Depending upon your available capital, you may wish to do this before you start selling franchises or after the entire program is put together.

Some business owners will try to handle the first few franchise sales transactions. This decision will depend upon several factors unique to your new franchise business.

Advertising for Franchisees. Use the advice of your franchise consultant to identify the most effective way to prospect for franchise candidates. Although your budget will play a role in this decision, be aware that there is no perfect ad program. You need to choose wisely and carefully measure results. Franchise advertising is not foolproof and you may have to try several vehicles before you find the most effective on a cost per franchise basis.

As you can see, there is a lot involved in starting up a new franchise and I only touched the surface. However, with the right business, sufficient capital and good advice, you'll be on your way to success.

Chapter 12

Selling Your Franchise

Sellers always think their business is worth more.

A typical objective of business owners, particularly small business owners, is to sell their business at some point in the future. After building a successful business and creating value, many decide to sell this asset to a third party or leave the business to their children.

I would say that in most cases, when it pertains to a franchise, the objective is typically to sell the business to a third party or back to the franchisor. In the case of a franchise, there are certain restrictions on how and to whom you can sell your franchise.

As previously mentioned, franchise agreements contain an assignment and transfer section, which sets forth the process by which a franchisee may assign and sell their business. These terms are not mutually exclusive. "Assignment" refers to the transfer of the franchise rights to a third party, and "the sale of the business" refers to the sale of the business itself. As an example, if you own a franchise and you've built up sales of $2 million per year and pay a royalty on those sales to the franchisor, you obviously own the business and you own the sales (although some service franchisors record the sales on their financial statements); however, those sales are generated subject to a franchise agreement. So, in a sense, you have a two-part ownership: the franchise and the business it generates. Although it is basically one transaction, you are selling your business and the franchise.

Therefore, as a franchisee, you can't sell your business without assigning the franchise agreement. In other words, you cannot sell a McDonald's, for example, to a third party, whereby they could open up Joe's Hamburger Stand. This is why I refer to the fact that the two components of the sale of your business are nonexclusive.

Some select franchisors may have a provision that requires you to sell the franchise back to them based upon a pre-existing formula. Generally, all franchisors that allow the franchisee to sell their franchise will retain a right of first refusal, which gives the franchisor the right to meet a "buyer's offer."

When you do decide that it's time to sell your business, I would suggest that you first identify what the value is for the specific kind of business you are engaged in and also remember that selling a franchise can be a doubled edged sword. By this, some franchises have strong branding and recognition that applies a significant value to that franchise.

Moreover, it could very well be a case where someone would like to own this franchise, but there are no more left in your territory. They might pay a premium for your franchise if you happen to be fortunate enough to be part of a system that has an extremely strong track record, high brand recognition, and good financial performance. On the other hand, you could be part of a franchise network that may not have strong brand recognition and where there are ample opportunities available to purchase a franchise from that same franchisor.

There may even be comparable franchise programs where an interested buyer may feel he or she has choices and would rather go that route rather than paying a premium for your existing franchise.

There are also instances where you have a combination of a brand that isn't necessarily critical to the success of the business because it is in an industry that has a significant amount of independent operators. You will sometimes find this in the temporary employment business where one can operate almost as successfully as the franchisee. This situation goes back to my previous experience.

An independent could provide their services that the franchisor would provide, but the independent wouldn't be obligated to pay a royalty for those services. Recall my prior comments where I spoke about the benefit of the services you are paying for. You will find that this will "come home to roost" when you decide to sell your business. You may have interested buyers who are not fully familiar with your franchise, but recognize the value of your business.

When they consider the fact that they are not only paying you for the business, but will be paying an ongoing royalty, I can assure you they are going to put their numbers together to make sure they are getting the right value. They will want the opportunity to achieve earnings in order to recover their investment and earn a profit.

My experience has been that the individual that is selling his or her business always thinks the business is worth more than others do. This is not to say that there aren't exceptions, but in general, franchisees and even independent business owners tend to place a higher value on that business than the potential buyer. Part of the reason is obvious. There is an emotional attachment to the business and because over a significant period of time the owner has built up that business and sees its benefits.

Be aware that an outside buyer will usually look at your business in a critical and financial way, more objectively than you do as the seller. A potential buyer will also look for ways to negotiate a lower price. Keep in mind, most individuals will not pay for potential because it is they who will do the job, not you. People will typically pay based upon current not future performance. I have been involved in a number of business acquisitions and sales. I've found the above to be typically the case.

The first step that you want to take is to identify a value for your business. There are many ways to do that. Some individuals have run blind ads in the business opportunity sections of their local newspapers or they have used brokers to place a value on their business. If you engage a broker, be very careful because you will be required to sign a sales agreement, which means that they will get a commission whether they sell it or someone else does. I always discouraged franchisees from engaging the services of a broker (my apology to that segment of our industry), because I felt that we could provide that service for them, and in some cases, the franchise sales people who worked for me would help find buyers for the franchisee. If that didn't work, then they would be urged to contact a broker. This really depends upon the unique situation with your franchisor and the services and support they can provide.

Some franchisors may simply have a "hands-off" approach when it comes to a franchisee finding a buyer.

Peter Barry, vice-president of franchising for ATC Medical Staffing Inc., a publicly owned franchise company, states, "Franchisees need to consider all options when they decide to sell their franchise. There is the traditional approach of advertising in the newspaper or on the Internet; however, franchisees should also consider selling to another franchisee or selling to a qualified individual within their own franchise organization. Franchisees should be aware of what options they have when they decide to sell their franchise." Barry adds, "The franchisee should contact their franchise department before taking the first steps."

Back to the subject of value, I think you want to find a way to establish a value and you have five different ways to do it. First, speak to the franchise salesperson and get a determination as to how they see the value of your business. Whether they are going to be totally accurate or not, hopefully you can get a "number" from them. Second, consider the industry that you are in and "what the multiples are," which refers to how the sale of the business is being calculated. Is it based upon a certain percentage of revenues or a multiple of earnings? Third, speak to your financial advisor or accountant who should be familiar with business transactions and should have some sense as to how to value your business. Fourth, you could speak to some fellow franchisees that recently sold or are looking to sell to get some sense of value, as to what the multiples are and what the businesses are selling for. Fifth, probably the simplest thing to do is to run a blind ad in the business opportunity section of your newspaper and see what kind of interest there is in your business. I caution you to be careful about this approach since the last thing you want is for your employees to know that you are selling your business. This may not be a problem, but most franchisees will cautiously guard their privacy when they decide to sell their business since some key employees might get nervous and leave.

Once you have determined a value for the business, the next step is to solicit buyers. First of all, I would contact the franchisor to see if they have any interest in your business. Frequently, we had franchise candidates who were interested in a specific territory which had already been franchised and these candidates would ask or request us to notify them if we should ever hear of that franchisee wanting to sell. Therefore, I would definitely contact the franchisor first and speak to your franchise sales department and let them know that you are considering selling and see if they have anyone interested in your market or territory.

Keep in mind that within the assignment and transfer section of your franchise agreement, the franchisor will retain a right of first refusal. What this means is that if you find a buyer for your franchise, you are required to obtain the consent of the franchisor in writing and that consent is absolutely required for you to sell that business. If you try to sell your franchise without the consent of the franchisor, then that sale will be "set aside" and the transaction canceled. All of this leads to this right of first refusal, which basically gives the franchisor the right to buy your business upon the same terms and conditions that you were offered.

Let's assume that someone offers to pay you $100,000 for your business in the form of $50,000 cash and a $50,000 note with interest over a one-year period. You are obligated to provide that information and those terms to the franchisor and they will have a period of time, thirty to sixty days, to either exercise or waive their right of first refusal. If the franchisor does exercise their right of first refusal, you'll receive the same value and terms as you would from your buyer.

This should not inhibit any franchisee from selling their business, because it really gives you the same value that you would have had if you sold it to a third party. Once again, I don't think that you are losing anything if you do have a bona fide buyer with an offer, since the franchisor has to meet the same terms and conditions as the offer that you received. You want to make sure that once you put your business on the market either utilizing the services of the franchisor, running ads, or using a business broker, keep in mind that the ultimate transaction will require the consent of the franchisor.

One point that I would like to make is that I have found in my experience that most franchisors will not offer to pay as much for a franchise as third parties. Unless there is a unique attribute to the business such as a large territory that has significant value which could be broken up into two or three other territories, you won't get the same kind of offer as you would from a third party. This is not to say that this is the case in every franchise company, but my position in the companies that I have been involved with was to tell our franchisees that we would be willing to make an offer although it may not be at a price level that they could possibly receive from a third party. Of course, having the right of first refusal provides the franchisor the option to make an offer at the beginning or wait.

Since most franchisors are in the business of franchising they may not have any interest in operating company outlets. However, if the price is right, then they may be persuaded. In fact, typically what we would do if we did purchase a franchise would be to try to find a franchisee to franchise it. This is the main reason that you will find many franchisors, unless they have a large corporate network, will offer you less than what you may be able to get from a third party.

Let's assume that you have identified a price for your business and you are ready to solicit candidates. The next step in this process is to utilize your attorney. You should never sell your business, nor should you buy one for that matter, without having your attorney represent you.

It is very important that you are protected when you sell your business. Not long ago, I had called up a franchisee of a large service franchisor. The franchisee had done work for me as a customer and I found out that there were new owners of the business. I asked them if they had a copy of the work that had been done for me and the new owner said, "Unfortunately, I don't because the former franchisee took everything with them." I asked him if there was any language in his agreement to protect the information that was part of the business. The new owner said, "No, we made a mistake. We should have had an attorney put language in the agreement that would have protected us." They didn't even have a noncompete in their agreement. They simply bought the franchise from the former franchisee who took certain information and could open and compete against the new owners as an independent. Their only protection was the franchisor's "noncompete" against the former franchisee.

This is only one example of why you need to have an attorney to advise you and work with you as you go through these transactions. It is very important that you protect yourself. There are a number of aspects to a sales agreement, especially when one is selling a business.

Any buyer is going to want to perform due diligence, which means that the buyer will want to see certain financial records and talk to the customers. Depending upon your financial structure, they may want to see corporate tax returns, depending once again on how you file your business reports. They will want to see financial records, sales registers, etc.

You need to be sure that a prospective buyer that will be privy to this kind of information, signs a confidentiality nondisclosure and possibly a nonsolicitation agreement. I realize that this is a "mouthful"; however, you will need some agreement that they will sign that protects you so that they cannot take that information and use it for their own benefit. Just remember, that they are going to learn something about your business and you want to be very careful in terms of what you convey to them and how serious they are about buying your business. Hopefully you have qualified them and determined that they are a bona fide buyer.

Along with this process, let's not forget that they are buying a franchise and they are assuming franchise rights. In most cases, they will be required to execute the current form of franchise agreement, which means that they need to be disclosed with the current UFOC.

It is very important to keep the franchisor in the loop and I would do this in writing and make sure that you understand the process that they have for a franchisee selling their franchise. In all of my companies, I had checklists so that if a franchisee called up and needed information for assigning their franchise to a new corporation, or selling to a third party I could forward them the information. In a few pages, I was able to explain what they had to do and what their obligations were and what we did and the role we played in the transaction. Make sure you keep the franchisor involved in this process so they are aware of what you are doing.

The due diligence, which a qualified buyer is going to perform, will involve meeting your people. Be very careful. You need to protect and guide your people, and of course, this leads into this sticky area of your key employees not wanting to leave the franchise. If they do, perhaps they could take revenues, depending upon the kind of business you are in and the size of the business. You want to be very careful about "opening your books," so to speak, and disclosing all of your operational practices and information regarding your business.

Once you have settled on a bona fide offer and qualified buyer for your business and have worked out the terms, etc., the franchisor representative is going to want to meet this buyer. As part of the assignment transfer requirement, the franchisor has the right to approve the candidate. Now, this is a very touchy area. Let me explain why. Let's assume that you have a franchise that is doing well and you want to sell it and you find a candidate that is interested in buying it. The franchisor has to approve that candidate as part of this process.

The franchisor will interview and meet the candidate. If they do not feel that the person is qualified, for whatever reason, they may find a way to disqualify them. Suddenly, you have lost your bona fide buyer. Now you have a few choices. You could go to the franchisor and say, "I had planned on selling this business," and they may say that they are interested but not at the purchase price you are looking for; or they may say, "We are not interested," which means that you will have to go through the process again and find anther buyer. If they deem the next buyer not to be qualified, suddenly you could find yourself in a "box."

Now, you have to protect yourself, because you could find that what you thought would be a certain price for your business isn't there. You might have to get your attorney involved depending upon the qualifications of your buyers. Although uncommon, there have been instances where a franchisor disqualified a buyer in order to position the franchisee to sell to the franchisor at a lower price. A good way to prevent this from happening is to have any prospective buyer complete a franchise application, which you can then forward to the franchisor. This approach (assuming the buyer has qualifications comparable to other franchisees in the network) can make it more difficult for the franchisor to turn down a qualified buyer. The sale and purchase of a business can be a very complex process. In the case of a franchise business the process becomes a bit more complicated. Be sure that before you are ready to sell your business, you know the requirements of your franchise agreement and the qualifications that franchisor expects the buyer to have. Above all, have sound and qualified professional advice.

CHAPTER 13

The Secrets to Success

*Although each franchise was different there were
certain characteristics and attributes that the
successful franchisees shared.*

Now that you have completed your journey through the
world of franchising, I hope that you have learned how to identify
and evaluate the right franchise for you. My objective for writing
this book was to share my years of experience in franchising with
prospective franchisees.

I've been very fortunate to have been a part of the franchising
industry and will continue participating in this very exciting and
dynamic industry. I also recognize how important successful
franchisees are to this industry. Whether one works as a franchisee
or franchisor, all of us recognize that every time a franchisee fails,
it impacts each of us in some way. Even those who have been
critical of the franchise industry, and particular franchisors,
acknowledge that the success rate of franchisees is still far above
that for independent businesses.

When you choose the franchise that appeals to you, make sure that you go through the right process and the franchise is the one that you not only feel confident in being able to operate, but that you have the experience and capital to make it a successful business.

There are a lot of so-called hot franchise and business opportunities in the market place; however, you need to be sure that you are not seduced by an opportunity that is not the right one for you.

Throughout my franchise career, I have worked in a number of franchise companies. Each of these companies was unique in that the franchise was very different. On numerous occasions, prospective franchisees would ask the question, "What does it take to be successful in operating this franchise?" Since each company was different, my response was specific to the requirements of that particular franchise operation.

In retrospect, although each franchise was different there were certain attributes or characteristics that all successful franchisees shared. This was true among each of the companies I worked with regardless of how different the franchise was.

I would like to present those traits that these successful franchisees shared.

Qualified for the Franchise Business—Each of the successful franchisees had a grasp or basic understanding of the franchise business. Whether it was a combination of matching business skills and experience to the franchise coupled with the right due diligence, these franchisees were able to assimilate into the franchise operation quite easily. I would hope that when you make your choice that you keep this fundamental point in mind.

Focus and Commitment—The successful franchisees were highly committed to their business. They maintained a focus of attention to the details of their business, which also served to provide them an understanding of how the business operated down to the most basic details. With rare exceptions, it's very difficult for a franchisee to be knowledgeable about their entire franchise operation without having a great deal of focus on their business. Of course, the opposite of this are those who are not focused and as a result, are not aware of what it takes to operate a successful franchise.

Active Involvement in the Business—Not to be confused with the previous attribute of "focus," the successful franchisees are actively involved in their business. However, an interesting point to be made is that these same individuals tend to have well-trained, competent, and motivated staff. My countless observations of successful franchisees reveal not only a highly active role in their business but also that they had an excellent team of people who not only supported the franchisee but could staff future expansion. Typically, they had an incentive or bonus program for their staff. Does it mean that this active participation in the business was a requirement for success? Not necessarily, but it sure increased the probability for success. I can recall one CEO I worked for who had a credo "as soon as I walk into a franchise location I can tell how successful they are based upon the level of activity in the location." He would say it's like there is "electricity in the air."

Awareness of Competition—This group would always be aware of their competitors. If I were to call about their marketplace and competition, the successful franchisees, regardless of the type of franchise business they were in, knew the answers. In point of fact I often found these people would call their franchisor representative or even senior management to make the franchisor aware of key market changes. Once again, the converse would be those franchisees that weren't aware of certain market factors. I can recall, in some cases, these individuals finding out after it was too late and after having lost sales. An awareness of competition is an important factor in any business operation. In your case, it's one more trait that the successful franchisees share.

Knowledge of the Franchise Network—The more successful franchisees are interested and show concern for the overall success of the franchise network. Rather than having their head in the sand, these individuals find the time to have a reading on how well the network is doing. If the franchise network is large, then these franchisees will at the very least stay in touch with network events within their own geographic region. This awareness and interest flows from the very same traits and attributes that I've already described. It's a manifestation of the interest these people have in their business.

Maintain Communication with the Franchisor—The successful franchisees find a way to maintain a dialog with the franchisor in good times and bad. I've experienced so many situations when my more successful franchisees would make a point to "stay in touch" with us. This is a reason why these same people are usually the ones who get called by their peers during troubled times. The other franchisees know that more successful franchisees are, by their results and efforts, in touch with what is going on in the network.

Leadership and Commitment to the Network—I've found that more successful franchisees have a strong commitment and affinity toward the franchise network. Regardless of the innate leadership skills these particular franchisees may have, their loyalty to the network causes them to rise to the occasion when necessary. In some cases, I've even been somewhat surprised by some of these franchisees whereby they took the initiative during troubled times to emerge in a leadership role on behalf of their fellow franchisees.

These attributes are what I have come to observe as being common among the more successful franchisees that I have encountered throughout my career. It doesn't mean that a franchisee must, in fact, possess all of these traits or attributes to be successful; however, I haven't met many successful franchisees in my career that didn't possess these traits.

I firmly believe that if you follow the advice and suggestions in this book, you'll have a head start toward becoming a successful franchisee. This path to success starts with choosing the right franchise based upon your experience, capital, and commitment to success.

CHAPTER 14

For the Franchisor

*Just as there are particular attributes that
successful franchisees have in common, so too can
the same be said for those franchisors that have
maintained a successful franchise
program over time.*

I have devoted the previous chapters to prospective franchisees and franchisors. I would be remiss if I failed to devote some part of this book to existing franchisors. After spending the majority of my franchise career as a franchise executive for various franchisors, I have come to recognize those attributes that successful franchisors share.

However, I would suggest that the chapters in this book that are directed to prospective franchisees could serve as a source of information and reflection by existing franchisors.

Since the material is designed for the new franchisee, a bit of role reversal by existing franchisors could be useful in terms of evaluating their current franchise program.

I recommend that existing franchisors review the questions in certain chapters and evaluate their responses as if they were asked all those same questions. I feel it could be helpful and pertinent to their franchise sales program.

Just as there are particular attributes that successful franchisees have in common so too can the same be said for those franchisors that have maintained a successful franchise program over time. I realize that success can be measured in many ways. Some may use growth in outlets, number of units in operation or some other factor. My approach is to apply certain characteristics to this subject. Some may take issue with these factors; however, they represent my own opinion based upon my experience.

I think you'll find these quite appropriate:

Profitable Franchise Program—The franchise program when properly operated is profitable. This does not mean that the franchisees must achieve extraordinary revenues but rather operate at average sales levels and be profitable. Investment requirements are consistent with presentations in the UFOC.

Consistent Track Record—There is a consistent history of successful performance by the franchise system. This means that over a period of time the franchise program has produced a preponderance of profitable franchisees.

The Franchise Resale Program Is Strong—One of the best attributes of a vibrant and successful franchise program is a demand for acquiring existing franchise locations. In the reverse, franchisees that find it difficult to sell their franchise business can usually attribute that fact to a weak franchise program.

Franchisor/Franchisee Relations Are Positive—The successful franchisors have good relations with their franchisees. Litigation is not excessive in relation to the size of the franchise network. I've yet to see litigation as a metric used to evaluate a franchisor. However, a review of the litigation history will often tell a story. If the preponderance of the litigation is brought by the franchisees it could indicate systemic problems with the franchise program.

Franchisees and franchisor executives have an ongoing dialog and are able to settle any major issues. Most likely there is a franchise advisory council in place, which meets on a regular basis. There are franchisee surveys conducted by the franchisor or third parties which can measure franchisee satisfaction levels.

The Franchise Network Is Growing—There is a consistent growth in new franchise locations. This indicates ongoing demand for the franchise opportunity, which is reflective of a successful franchise. I would not use growth in the short term such as two years or less as an indicator but rather growth over a minimum of at least three years.

These are the attributes I consider to be indicative of successful franchisors. I certainly recognize that the best measure is when both franchisor and franchisee are profitable. I feel that the other items complete the circle.

CHAPTER 15

The Laws of Franchising

A wounded franchisee is a dangerous franchisee.

After spending over twenty-five years in the franchise industry as both franchisor and franchisee, I've had the opportunity to observe over one thousand franchisees in various stages of activity. Since most of this time was spent as a franchise executive with responsibility for franchise operations, I was keenly aware of the issues, challenges, and behavior of countless franchisees. These experiences provided me the opportunity to form a set of principles regarding franchising and the interaction between franchisors and franchisees.

The beginning of this concept started during a staff meeting with other executives from my company. It was reported that a large number of franchisees were complaining about a particular matter. When the president of my company asked me to comment on this issue, I responded with a bit of dramatic flair, "Teixeira's first law of franchising states that when most franchisees complain about the same thing they are usually right."

In due course, I developed several other "laws" and within my company became known among my fellow executives for this particular penchant.

As time went on, I recognized that there was a particular pattern of behavior that exists in most franchise companies. I soon developed these observations into what I've come to call "The Laws of Franchising." I have developed these laws after observing numerous activities and events during my twenty-five years in the franchise industry.

I would like to take this opportunity to share my laws with you. Keep in mind that I base these "laws" on a significant amount of experience, flavored with a dash of personal opinion. As you read them, I think you'll find them quite interesting and for those familiar with franchising that they strike a familiar chord.

1. The franchise agreement must favor the franchisor in order to maintain stability.

The franchise agreement must be strong enough so that system standards and quality can be maintained. If the franchisor doesn't have the tools necessary to enforce and maintain system standards than the entire franchise network can be harmed. A strong franchise agreement will protect the good franchisees from the bad.

As I've indicated in previous chapters, a strong franchise agreement is a prerequisite for upholding and maintaining standards within the franchise network. If McDonald's didn't have the right franchise agreement to provide them the tools to defend and protect their credo "QSVC" (quality, service, value and cleanliness), I doubt that they would have been able to achieve consistent operations throughout the United States and overseas. Consider that a major reason for the success of McDonald's was that whenever you visit a McDonald's you knew what to expect and you usually received it with very few exceptions.

2. Never limit a franchisee's ability to earn more money.

When a franchisor limits the earning capabilities of a franchisee by limiting territory, expansion opportunities, or through some other vehicle, then there is a high probability that better franchisees will either leave the system or lack incentive.

Some franchisors feel that allowing franchisees to become financially powerful could cause problems for the franchisor. In point of fact, my experience has been that highly successful franchisees are usually less of a problem and threat than those franchisees who are doing poorly or who are unprofitable. The poorly performing franchisees have a lot less to lose and some may even feel threatened so litigation against the franchisor may be the strategy of choice for this group.

Limiting or inhibiting the earning power of franchisees runs counter to stimulating the entrepreneurial spirit of the franchisee and quite frankly is contrary to the very principles that the franchise industry was built upon.

Without exception, I have found that franchisees that are given the opportunity to continue to reach for higher goals presented me with very few problems. Of course, if the franchisor failed to fulfill its basic contractual obligations that was an entirely different matter. Yet, even in that situation I still found the larger franchisees easier to deal with.

3. Franchisees must relate to successful franchisees.

The franchisor must use those techniques at its disposal to encourage its franchisees to identify with and relate to the successful franchisees in the network.

By utilizing bulletins, meetings, newsletters, and awards to recognize those franchisees that have performed the best, there is less likelihood that the franchisees will refer to any malcontents for advice and guidance.

There will be certain times during the maturation of a franchise system when problems can arise. In some cases, the franchise network may be growing faster than the franchisor is capable of servicing. There may even be logistical problems that a franchisor is facing during early periods of its growth. In these cases, franchisees may be drawn to those franchisees that are the most vocal and difficult to deal with. In my experience this group does not usually include the successful franchisees.

Although franchisees will gravitate toward their more successful colleagues over time, the franchisor should do all in its power to encourage these relationships.

4. Franchisees will always place their own security first.

A franchisee will always consider their own security and the security of their business first when taking action that involves their relationship with the franchisor. It goes without saying that franchisees will be very cautious when they find themselves in a position where their business and franchise is threatened.

Now this may appear to be a contradiction of my previous comments regarding the successful and larger franchisees being easier to deal with yet it isn't. The reason is simple: when a franchisee faces the choice between the security of their business versus loyalty to the franchisor, they will defend and protect their business.

During my career, I have witnessed situations where a franchisor faced financial hardship, which impacted the performance of its franchisees. Despite the willingness of its franchisees to work with the franchisor, several of them chose to take a firm stand in order to protect their business.

Some tried to exit the system legally others simply dropped out. The bottom line is that they did what they felt was necessary to save their business even if it led to litigation.

When a franchisor encounters a franchisee that is overly anxious or critical regarding a particular situation it must be recognized that the franchisee may be concerned with self-preservation.

5. *Most franchisees will avoid criticizing the franchisor directly.*

Most franchisees are very careful to avoid directly criticizing
or confronting the franchisor. Since many franchisees fear the
power of the franchisor or because they may require a concession
from the franchisor in the future a franchisee may be unwilling
to make a direct critique.

Franchisees will seek out peers and/or the franchise advisory
council as a way to offer comments. Regardless of how strong
the relationship is between a franchisor and its franchisees most
franchisees will be very cautious in finding fault with the franchisor
on a direct basis.

Obviously, this is not always the case and exceptions will
arise in terms of the more successful franchisees; however, most
franchisees do not wish to be typecast as troublemakers or
complainers.

Franchisors should take note of this fact when they are seeking
feedback or measuring the state of franchise relations in the
network. In many cases, franchisees will complain to each other
about the franchisor who may not be aware of existing or potential
problems.

The use of surveys and direct reports from franchisor field
staff is a method for the franchisor to gain feedback despite the
reluctance of most franchisees to complain directly.

6. *Franchisors should avoid disputes that they are not willing to fight for.*

I have personally seen countless situations where a franchisor
took a strong position regarding a particular issue only to relent
under pressure from their franchisees.

There are two dynamics at play regarding this situation:
First, the franchisor may fail to properly analyze its position
from a contractual standpoint in terms of how their position
would be received by its franchisees. As an example, the

franchisor may be relying upon a provision in the franchise agreement that may have some ambiguity regarding the specific matter in dispute and the franchisor may not have fulfilled all of its obligations under the franchise agreement, which the franchisees now demand the franchisor to comply with. Secondly, the particular "position" that the franchisor has taken may have such impact upon the franchisees, whether actual or perceived, that the franchisees unite against it. The franchisor may "win the battle but lose the war."

If the franchisor takes a strong stand, then it must be very careful to assess the impact from a franchise relation's standpoint.

There are situations where a franchisor may choose a course of action, which requires a resolute stand. However, the franchisor must be careful to prepare their position and have an expectation regarding the response from its franchisees and be willing to deal with that response.

7. *Franchisees abhor a vacuum and will join together to fill one.*

Franchisees, like any other group, require and seek affiliation and association with others. When a franchisor fails to stay involved with its franchisees and doesn't maintain contact, then the franchisees will seek each other out in order to offer support, exchange feedback, and bond among themselves.

I have seen this happen in a particular company where the franchisor was over one thousand miles away and tended to avoid the geographically distant franchisees versus those closer to "home." The result was a group of franchisees that formed a quasi-association, which eventually served as a source of irritation and problems for the franchisor.

This situation can be avoided if the franchisor through its representatives, communication vehicles, and regional and national meetings maintains a degree of contact with all of its franchisees. Failure to do so will create a vacuum, and like nature, franchisees abhor a vacuum.

8. *When franchisees complain about the same thing they are usually right.*

My first "law" has been proven to be true time and time again. The most surprising aspect regarding this "law" is how many times a franchisor will hear of complaints or issues from their franchisees and either deny it's a problem or totally ignore the franchisees.

It's really a matter of common sense that when a large number of franchisees recite the same complaint, there must be some truth to it.

This does not mean that the franchisor should react with panic every time there are complaints from their franchisees. What it does mean is that the franchisor had better pay attention if the majority of their franchisees raise the same issue.

I can recall a situation in one of the companies that I worked for. There was a change in operating procedures that had been implemented without much fanfare. After about a month, I started to receive reports from my field staff that many of their franchisees were complaining about this new procedure.

Fortunately, I was able to gather the information rather quickly and after reporting the situation to the president of the company I was able to head off a confrontation with our franchisees over this issue. We anticipated the potential outcome of this problem and made adjustments to the new procedure. Had we ignored the complaints or simply waited, we would have had to make the change anyway; however, we would have lost valuable credibility with our franchisees.

9. *The most dangerous franchisee is a wounded franchisee.*

During my franchise career, I have found that the franchisee who is struggling and/or has not performed very well may be more willing to litigate against the franchisor than their more successful peers. The franchisee who faces failure has virtually very little to lose compared to the franchisee who operates a profitable franchise.

The successful and profitable franchisee has a business, which has value and is capable of being sold if necessary. Contrast this situation with the struggling or problematic franchisee that may face the loss of their investment.

Although not true in every case, it's a sure bet that this situation if not addressed will deteriorate over time. The moral of the lesson is to pay attention to all of your franchisees, be well documented, and stay in communication with struggling franchisees. Finally, have a game plan for dealing with those franchisees that aren't performing as expected. This could be a buyback, financial assistance, or a documented action plan delivered to the franchisee.

10. Franchisors must never be surprised by the actions of their franchisees.

My final "law" is a requirement for all franchisors to subscribe to. The simple truth is that franchisors must be aware of what is taking place within their franchise system. Benign neglect will only lead to problems in the future.

I recall being on a teleconference call with a group of franchisees that were part of a separate franchise division of my company. After the introductory comments by the division manager, there was a chorus of complaints from one franchisee after another.

It was obvious to those of us in senior management that the division head had been caught off guard and had not expected the deluge of criticism from the franchisees.

This situation arose because the franchisor representatives did not have their finger on the pulse of the franchisees. There is an abundance of literature on the subject of franchise relations. A failure to follow these practices will lead to problems at some point in time. One of my frequent quotes as a franchise executive was, "I don't like surprises because they are usually bad."

If the franchisor is "surprised" by certain events or actions on the part of its franchisees, this clearly demonstrates a weakness on the part of the franchisor.

By contacts with its franchisees via field representatives, executive phone calls to those franchisees who tend to be "tuned in" to the network, conference calls, surveys or other means, the franchisor will protect itself from being "surprised."

These are my "Laws of Franchising" and represent years of experience observing and dealing with franchisees. Like anything else, there are exceptions; however, I can say with complete confidence that these "laws" will usually run true to form.

CHAPTER 16

Going International

*The financial rewards and sense of
accomplishment from transacting with a licensee
in another country can be a
rewarding experience.*

Today, franchising is truly an international phenomenon.
From Thailand to Mauritius one will find a franchise. It wasn't
that many years ago when U.S. franchisors would focus on western
Europe and a few other regions of the world.

For a number of reasons, many countries received little or no
attention from franchisors. Since that time, franchising has
penetrated virtually every developed country in the world albeit
some more than others. There are thirty-four franchise associations
throughout the world. From Kazakhstan to Argentina to South
Africa to Malaysia, the franchise industry is well represented.

With the advent of the Internet and the rapid availability of
information, more and more of the world's population have
become aware of franchise brands and their popularity. This

increase in information has accelerated the growth of international franchising by creating a higher level of awareness on the part of entrepreneurs throughout the world.

International franchise opportunities are available for qualified franchisors. In fact, these opportunities exist for large franchisors that may have limited territories left in their home country and smaller franchisors that desire to export their franchise to other countries. The primary method for establishing a franchise in another country is to grant a license to a qualified and properly capitalized entity.

This arrangement consists of the franchisor contracting with an individual or group in the foreign country under a master license agreement. Under this agreement the licensee pays a fee to the franchisor that is established by estimating the number of potential locations in the country multiplied by a unit franchise fee. A master license fee could range from $200,000 to over $1,000,000. I have done transactions with fees at various levels.

In addition to the master license fee, the franchisor will usually receive a royalty on licensee sales, which represents a percentage of the franchise fee that the licensee charges its franchisees. As an example, if the licensee charges an 8 percent royalty the licensee may remit 2 percent to the franchisor. Obviously, these figures are negotiated between the franchisor and the licensee and as such can vary among transactions.

The role that the licensee plays in their own country is as franchisor. As such the licensee is responsible for selling franchises, training, maintaining standards, and supporting the system. The franchisor will provide training, support the licensee, provide enhancements to the franchise program and conduct audits to maintain compliance with franchise standards.

There is a great deal more to the relationship; however, these are the key elements of the franchisor and foreign licensee transaction.

For franchisors that want to go international, the benefits can be exciting. Having done a number of international transactions I can attest to this fact firsthand.

Some of these benefits include:

- Additional sales and profits
- Added exposure and credibility for the franchisor
- Franchise program enhancements resulting from operations in other countries
- Added enthusiasm generated among the franchisor and its franchisees
- For public franchise companies, increased interest on the part of the investor community

For franchisors that desire to enter international markets, there are a number of key steps that need to be followed. If the results of this process are positive, then the next step is to establish an action plan for recruiting licensee candidates.

1. Quality Franchise Program—You need to have a solid franchise program that rests upon a foundation of solid results. This doesn't mean that the franchisor must be of a specific size although I would expect a minimum of fifty franchise locations.

2. Committed Franchise Organization—The franchisor executives particularly at the top must understand and be committed to the international venture. Without this commitment members of the franchisor organization may not follow up and support the project as required.

   All of the international transactions that I have done with various franchisors had the involvement and support of the president of those companies.

3. Resources in Place—The franchisor must have the capital and human resources needed to go international. This includes up-to-date manuals, marketing materials, applicable supplier and product procurement standards, and training programs. Since the licensee will most likely require a franchisor representative to be on site during the pre- and post-opening of the first location, there

should be an individual available to fulfill this role for the franchisor.

4. Register Your Marks and Protect Your Domain Name— You'll need to have your "marks" properly registered prior to entering the new country and protect your intellectual property. Engage a trademark attorney to advise you and perform this function.

5. Conduct Some Research—Be sure to invest some time in researching the country or countries that have your interest. I would suggest a visit to the home page of the U.S. Commercial Service *www.export.gov,* which contains a veritable wealth of information on countries throughout the world. There are a number of services, which "commerce" offers from posting your site to recruiting licensees.

    This site can lead you to country summaries and research reports. A review of the Internet can yield country-by-country information in the form of press releases, articles, studies, and news items.

6. Engage the Services of a Qualified Consultant—If you're serious in taking your company international, then be sure to obtain advice from someone who has done international transactions and has visited a number of countries. You want to rely upon experts who have prospected candidates, negotiated agreements, and have operational experience with these transactions. Taking a franchise international can be an exciting and dramatic step for a franchisor. The financial rewards and sense of accomplishment from transacting with a licensee in another country is an exciting experience.

I've been fortunate to do transactions in Europe, Asia, and South America. The personal satisfaction and sense of professional accomplishment from these transactions were among the high points of my business career. It's an exciting endeavor for a franchisor. The important point is to be qualified and committed to international operations.

EPILOGUE

As the franchise industry continues to grow throughout the world, it is now emerging in the world's largest country. China, waking up from a long economic sleep, has come to recognize the benefits of franchising. This recognition is being spurned by a thirst for consumer products, encouragement from the Chinese government, and by many of its citizens who embrace the franchising concept.

This news is not surprising given China's entry into the World Trade Organization coupled with its desire to join the world's modern economic club.

As people continue to seek franchise opportunities, the availability of information especially through the Internet offers the franchise candidate the ability to learn about franchise offerings in less time. It will not be too long when the UFOC will be delivered via e-mail to the majority of franchise prospects. However, with this surge of franchise information and growth comes the opportunity for unscrupulous franchisors to take advantage. There is no substitute for exercising good judgment when seeking a franchise.

The information that I presented in this book is based upon my real-life experiences. It represents over twenty-five years of dealing with franchisees from the United States and many other countries. I was fortunate to work for a number of franchisors who, regardless of their shortcomings, all shared an abiding belief in the power of franchising. I had the enviable experience to attend countless franchise conventions where I was able to acknowledge and recognize franchisees for achieving noteworthy accomplishments. It was these events that provided me the greatest amount of satisfaction. To be able to reward franchisees for their accomplishments.

Although many received a simple plaque, I could see their joy in being recognized before their peers. Perhaps it is this fact that most clearly exemplifies the essence of franchising. It is an industry that allows individuals to own and operate their own business with the opportunity to be as successful as they want. I say this knowing that franchising, not unlike other institutions, is imperfect. However, there are certainly enough franchise opportunities to satisfy the entrepreneurial spirit that stirs in so many.

A recent report "Economic Impact of Franchised Businesses" by the National Economic Consulting Practice of PricewaterhouseCoopers revealed some interesting facts:

Franchised businesses operated 767,483 establishments in the United States in 2001.

These establishments provided 9,797,117 jobs, met a $229.1 billion payroll, and produced $624.6 billion of output.

These businesses accounted for 3.2 percent of all U.S. business establishments.

Their economic activity accounted for

  7.4 percent of all private sector jobs;
  5.0 percent of all private sector payrolls; and
  3.9 percent of all private sector output.

Clearly, franchising is thriving in the United States and continues to become a significant export of the U.S. economy.

I'm sure, by the time this book is published, franchising will have recorded more milestones and its impact will continue to be felt in more and more countries.

As I embark on my new path of consulting new and existing franchisors, I will continue to draw upon the lessons that I learned from the many franchisors and franchisees that I've been associated with throughout my career.

Appendix

Franchise Contact Information:

IFA
International Franchise Association
1350 New York Avenue NW, Suite 900
Washington DC 20005-4709
(202) 628-8000
Fax: (202) 628-0812

FTC
Division of Marketing Practices
Bureau of Consumer Protection
Federal Trade Commission
6th Street and Pennsylvania Avenue NW
Washington DC 20580
(202) 326-3128

California
Commission of Corporations
Department of Corporations
1515 K Street, Suite 200,
Sacramento CA 95814
(916) 445-7205

Hawaii
Securities Examiner
Department of Commerce and Consumer Affairs
1010 Richards Street,
Honolulu HI 96813

Illinois
Chief, Franchise Bureau
Office of the Attorney-General
Rm 12-186
100 W. Randolph St.
Chicago IL 60601

Indiana
Chief Deputy Commissioner,
Franchise Section
Indiana Securities Division
Secretary of State
302 West Washington St., Rm E-111
Indianapolis IN 46204
(317) 232-6681

Maryland
Franchise Examiner
Office of the Attorney-General
Maryland Division of Securities
200 St. Paul Place
Baltimore MD 21202
(410) 576-7044

Michigan
Franchise Administrator
Consumer Protection Division
Office of the Attorney-General
PO Box 30213,
Lansing MI 48909

Minnesota
Franchise Examiner
Minnesota Department of Commerce
85 7th Place East, Suite 500,
St. Paul MN 55101
(615) 296-4026; Registration Div.
(651) 296-4520

New York
New York Department of Law
Bureau of Investor Protection and Securities
120 Broadway, 23rd Floor,
New York NY 10271
(212) 416-8000

North Dakota
Franchise Examiner
Office of Securities Commission
600 East Blvd., Dept 414
State Capitol, 5th Floor
Bismarck ND 58505
(701) 328-2910

Oregon
Department of Consumer and Business Services
Franchise and Corporate Securities Division
Labor and Industries Building,
350 Winter Street NE, Room 300
Salem OR 97301-3881
(503) 378-4140

Rhode Island
Chief Securities Examiner
Department of Business Regulation
Securities Division, Franchise Section
233 Richmond Street, Suite 232
Providence RI 02903-4232
(401) 222-3084

FranchiseKnowHow, LLC
PO Box 714
Stony Brook NY 11790 www.franchiseknowhow.com
631-246-5782

Farrell Fritz
EAB Plaza, 14th Floor, W. Tower
Uniondale NY 11556
516-745-0099

South Dakota
Franchise Administrator
Division of Securities
118 West Capitol Avenue
Pierre SD 57501-5070

Virginia
Chief Examiner
State Corporation Commission
Division of Securities and Retail Franchising
1300 E. Main Street, 9th Floor
Richmond VA 23219

Washington
Administrator
Dept of Financial Institutions
Securities Division
210 11ᵗʰ Avenue SW, Room 300
PO Box 9033
Olympia WA 98504-9033
(360) 902-8700

Wisconsin
Franchise Administrator
Securities and Franchise Registration
Wisconsin Securities Commission
345 West Washington, 3ʳᵈ Floor
PO Box 7846
Madison WI 53701
(608) 261-9555

Nixon Peabody, LLP
1818 Market Street, 11ᵗʰ Floor
Philadelphia, PA. 19103
215-246-3520

Mario C. Herman, Esq.
2987 Hope Mills Lane
Adamson MD 21710
(301) 607-4111

Franchise Search, Inc.,
48 Burd Street, Suite 101
Nyack NY 10960
845-727-3918

International Franchise Contact Information:

Argentina
Company Name: Argentine Association of Franchising
Address: Av. Libertardor 222, 70-A Buenos Aires
                          1001, Argentina
Contact Number: (54-11) 4-394-3318 or (54-11) 4-326-5499
Fax Number: (54-11) 4-394-8107
Web site: *http://www.aafranchising.com*
E-mail Address: *info@aafranchising.com*
Chairman: Mr. Lucas Secades
President: Mr. Jose Fernandez

Australia
Company Name: Franchise Council of Australia
Address: GPO Box 1498N, Melbourne Victoria 3001,
                          Australia
Contact Number: 1300 669030
Fax Number: 03 9822 7752
Web site: *info@franchise.org.au*
Chairman: Stephen Giles
CEO: Richard Events

Belgium
Company Name: European Federation of Franchising
Address: Ave Louise 179/14B-1050 Brussels, Belgium
Contact Number: (32-2) 520-1607
Fax Number: (32-2) 520-1735
Web site: *http://www.eff-franchise.com*
E-mail Address: *info@eff_franchise.com*
Chairman: Pierre Jeanmart
CEO: Carol Chopra

Brazil

Company Name:	Brazilian Association of Franchising
Address:	Av. Brigaderio Faria Lima, 1739-3 Andar CEP 01452-001, Jd. Paulistano 0 Sao Paulo—SP—Brazil
Contact Number:	+ 55.11.3814.4200
Fax Number:	+ 55.11.3817.5986
Web site:	*http://www.abf.com.br*
E-mail address:	*anette@abf.com.br*
Chairman:	Ricardo Young
President:	Mr. Gerson Keila
CEO:	Mrs. Anette Trompeter

United Kingdom

Company Name:	British Franchise Association
Address:	Thames View, Newton Road Henley-on-Thames Oxon RG9 1HG, United Kingdom
Contact Number:	(44) 1491-578-050
Fax Number:	(44) 1491-573-517
Web site:	*http://www.british-franchise.org.uk*
E-mail address:	*mailroom@british-franchise.org.uk*
Chairman:	Mr. Melvin Lusty
CEO:	Mr. Brian Smart

Canada

Company Name:	Canadian Franchise Association
Address:	2585 Skymark Avenue, Suite 300, Mississauga ON. L4W4L5, Canada
Contact Number:	+ 905.625.2896
Fax Number:	+ 905.625.9076
Web site:	*http://cfa.ca*
Chairman:	Mr. Sam Hamman
President:	Mr. Richard Cunningham

China

Company Name: China Chain Store and Franchise Association
Address: No. 25 Yuetan North Street Beijing 100834— PR China
Contact Number: (86 10) 6839-1474 or 1464
Fax Number: (86 10) 6839-1434 or 1444
Web-site: *www.ccfa.org.cn*
E-mail address: *lucywu@ccfa.org.cn*
Secretary: Ms. Lucy Wu Rui Ling

Germany

Company Name: German Franchise Association
Address: Luisentrasse, 41 10117 Berlin, Germany
Contact Number: + 49.0.30.278.90.20
Fax Number: + 49.0.30.278.90.215
Web site: *http://www.dfv-franchise.de*
E-mail Address: *info@dfv-franchise.de*
President: Mr. Manfred Maus (OBI)

Hong Kong

Company Name: Hong-Kong Franchise Association
Address: 11/F Unit A, United Centre, 96 Queensway, Hong Kong Queensway, Hong Kong
Contact Number: + 852.2529.9229
Fax Number: + 852.2527.9843
Web site: *http://www.franchise.org.hk*
E-mail Address: *hfka@franchise.org.hk*
Chairman: Y.K. Pang

India

Company Name: Indian Association of Franchising
Address: 54-A, Elite Auto House, Sir. M Vasanji Road, Chakala Andheri (East), Mumbai 400093 India
Contact Number: (91-22) 692 1258
E-mail Address: *fai@vsn1.net*
Chairman: C. Yoginer Pal
CEO: Ameet Sheth

Italy

Company Name: Italian Franchise Association
Address: Viale L. Majno, 42 IT—20129 Milan, Italy
Contact Number: (39 02) 29 00 37 79
Fax Number: (39 02) 65 55 919
Web site: *http://www.assofranchising.it*
E-mail Address: *assofranchising@assofranchising.it*
Chairman: Mr. Graziano Fiorelli

Japan

Company Name: Japan Franchise Association
Address: 2nd Akiyama Building Roranomon 3-6-2, Minato-ku Tokyo 105-0001, Japan
Contact Number: + 81.3.5777.8701
Fax Number: + 81.3.5777.8711
E-mail Address: *nibayashi@jfa-fc.or.jp*
CEO: Mr. Osamu Nibayashi

The Netherlands

Company Name: Netherlands Franchise Association
Address: Bloomberglaan 12 NL, 1217 RR Hilversum The Netherlands
Contact Number: + 31.35.624.23.00
Fax Number: + 31.35.624.91.94
Web site: *http://www.nfv.nl*
E-mail Address: *franchise@nfv.nl*
President: Mr. J. D. Vander Ent (Etos, bv)
CEO: Mr. Jos Burgers

New Zealand

Company Name: Franchise Association of New Zealand
Address: PO Box 23 364, Hunters Corner, Papatoetoe, Auckland, New Zealand
Contact Number: + 649.278.9012
Fax Number: + 649.278.9013
Web site: *http://www.franchise.org.nz*
E-mail Address: *contact@franchise.org.nz*
Chairman: Mr. Robert Fowler

Philippine

Company Name:	Philippine Franchise Association
Address:	701 OMM-Cittra Bldg. San Miguel Ave. Ortigas Center, Pasig City
Contact Number:	+ 623.687.0365—67
Fax Number:	+ 623.687.0635
Web site:	*pfa@nwave.net*
Chairman:	Mr. Samie Lim

Singapore

Company Name:	Franchising and Licensing Association, Singapore
Address:	Informatics Building, 5 International Business Park, Singapore 609914
Contact Number:	(65) 568 0802
Fax Number:	(65) 568 0722
E-mail Address:	*sifa@pacific.net.sg*
Chairman:	Dhirendra Shantilal

South Africa

Company Name:	Franchise Association of South Africa
Address:	24 Wellington Road, 2193 Houghton, South Africa
Contact Name:	(27-11) 484-1285
Fax Number:	(27-11) 484-1291
Web site:	*http://www.fasa.co.za*
E-mail Address:	*fasa@faza.co.za*
Chairman:	Mr. Mahesh Amarath
President:	Mr. Nic Louw

Spain

Company Name:	Spanish Association of Franchising
Address:	Avenida de las Ferias S/N Apda (POB) 476 46035 Valencia, Spain
Contact Number:	+ 34.96.386.11.23
Fax Number:	+ 34.96.363.61.11
Web site:	*http://www.fraquiciandores.com*
E-mail Address:	*aef@fieravalencia.com*
President:	Mr. Xavier Vallhonrat Llurba
CEO:	Mr. Edurado Abadia Gonzalez

Sweden

Company Name:	Swedish Association of Franchising
Address:	Massansgatan 18/ Box 5243 SE 40224 Goteborg, Sweden
Contact Number:	+ 46.31.83.69.43
Fax Number:	+ 46.31.81.10.72
Web site:	*http://www.franchiseforeningen.a.se*
E-mail Address:	*karin.franchiseforeningen@telia.com*
Chairman:	Mr. Anders Fernlund
President:	Mrs. Karin Kisker

Taiwan

Company Name:	Taiwan Chain Store and Franchise Association
Address:	7 F, NO 197 Nanking E Rd. Sec. 4 Taipe, Taiwan
Contact Number:	(8862) 2712 1250
Fax Number:	(8862) 2712 7997
Web site:	*http://www.tfca.org.tw*
E-mail Address:	*shirley.huang@tcfa.org.tw*

Franchise and Business Definitions

Acknowledgment of Receipt
It is the last page of the UFOC that you sign and return. It provides proof of the received UFOC.

Advertising Fee
A fee paid by the franchisee to the franchisor for co-op advertising expenditures. Not all franchisors charge advertising fees.

Agreement
The franchise agreement that you sign with a franchisor.

Amortization
The repayment of a loan by periodic payments of principal and interest.

Appraisal
Professional opinion or estimate of the value of property, in most states by licensed appraisers.

Approved Products
Products that a franchisee must purchase from the franchisor and approved suppliers.

Arbitration
The process in which an arbitrator hears both sides of a dispute and renders a decision. Compared to using the courts this process is usually less costly.

Area Development Rights
The rights granted to a franchisee to open a certain number of franchise locations within a specified geographic area within a certain time frame.

Asset Purchase and Sale Agreement
A contract that details the provisions under which a business may be sold.

Assets
Owned real or personal property that can be used for payment of debt.

Balance Sheet
A financial statement that gives an accounting picture of assets or property owned by a company and of claims against the assets or property on a given date.

Bankruptcy
An individual or organization unable to meet debt obligations petitions a federal district court for reorganization of debts or liquidation of assets or similar proceedings, or an involuntary petition is filed by creditors of the individual or organization.

Bridge Loan
A type of temporary financing, which is extended to a borrower until permanent financing is secured. At that time, funds from the new permanent financing are used to pay off the bridge loan.

Broker
A person involved in the sale and purchase of a business or property. Brokers represent either sellers or buyers.

Business Format Franchising
The franchisor licenses the franchisee to use the franchisor product, service, and trademarks and also teaches the franchisee the marketing, selling, financial, and personnel procedures. Most franchises are business format franchises.

Business Plan
A plan that provides the operational and financial details of a new business, including cash flow models and projections.

Collateral
Assets used as security for a lease/loan.

Consolidated Financial Statements
Statements that report the combined operating results, financial position, and cash flows of two or more legally separate but affiliated companies as if they were one economic entity.

Company-owned Outlet
Company-owned locations are owned and operated by the franchisor and similar in most respects to a franchise location.

Conversion Franchise
A franchise that was converted from an independent business to a franchise operation.

Copyright
The exclusive right of a person to use, and to license others to use works of creativity, a form of intellectual property. Examples are books, literature, etc.

Debt Service Coverage
Cash required in a given period for payment of interest and current principal.

Default
A failure to fulfill a provision, which is contained in a franchise agreement. Franchisee and franchisor may default.

Demographics
Macroeconomic information about a business, population, income, major traffic flows, etc.

Disclosure Document (Uniform Franchise Offering Circular)
Required by the Federal Trade Commission (FTC) and certain states to provide to prospective franchisees. Franchisors must give potential investors a basic disclosure document at the earlier of the first face-to-face meeting or ten business days before any money is paid or an agreement is signed in connection with the franchise.

Distributorship
A right granted by a manufacturer to sell a product to others. A distributorship is not a franchise. However, certain distributorship arrangements may qualify as a franchise or as a business opportunity requiring disclosure.

Earnings Claims
Representation by the franchisor pertaining to the sales or earnings performance of the franchisees. Must conform to section 19 of the UFOC.

EBITDA
Earnings before interest, taxes, depreciation, and amortization. EBITDA is a measure of the cash flow available to make debt payments.

Exclusive Territory
An exclusive territory right gives you as the franchisee the right to that territory. The franchisor cannot sell other franchises within that territory. May also relate to products or services sold in the territory.

Federal Trade Commission
The U.S. government agency that regulates interstate commerce, franchising, and other business activities.

Financial Statements (F/S)
Consists of two parts, a balance sheet, and a profit and loss or income statement.

- A balance sheet states how much a business is worth.
  (Assets - Liabilities = Equity or Net Worth)
- A P&L statement shows how much a business makes.
  (Sales - Costs = Profits or Income)

Franchise

A business in which the owner (franchisor) of a product, service, or method obtains distribution through affiliated dealers (franchisees) and offers assistance in such areas as operations, training, marketing, and managing in return for a consideration.

Franchise Agreement

A written contract between the franchisor and the franchisee detailing the specifics of operations using the franchisor proprietary items, logos, etc.

Franchise Fee

The initial fee paid by the franchisee to the franchisor to obtain the franchise rights.

Franchisee

A person or entity to whom the right to conduct a business is granted by the franchisor.

Franchising

A method of doing business within a given industry where parties are involved in franchising: the franchisor and the franchisee.

Franchisor

A person or entity issuing or granting a franchise or license.

Gross Sales

Revenue before any adjustments, taxes, or expenses are deducted.

Initial Investment

The initial franchise fee and the total investment amount including working capital necessary to open a franchise.

International Franchise Association (IFA)

The international trade organization for franchisor and franchisees. Based in Washington DC, the IFA requires a rigid code of ethics to be followed by member franchisor.

Limited Liability Company (LLC)

A limited liability company is a business structure best described as a hybrid between a partnership and a corporation— a "pass through" of all profits and losses to the owners without taxation of the entity itself, as in a partnership, and a shield from personal liability, as in a corporation.

Line of Credit (LOC)

A loan that may be borrowed against and paid down during its term. These loans usually have a covenant / special condition attached stating that the loan must have a zero balance for a specified period of time.

Master Franchisee

An individual or company having the exclusive rights to develop a particular territory by selling franchises in the same territory.

Multilevel Marketing (MLM)

A form of distributorship in which you receive commission on your own sales and on the sales of those whom you sign up as distributors.

Noncompete Clause

A clause in a contract that prohibits a person from entering into the same line of business for a specific period of time. This will apply after an employment or termination agreement is signed.

Nonsolicitation

Provision, which requires a former franchisee or employee form soliciting the franchisor employees or clients for a specific term.

Offer

The proposal to sell a franchise to a prospective franchisee.

Operations Manual

The manual(s), which instruct a franchisee on how to operate the franchised business and covers all aspects of the business, including general business procedures. May consist of different manuals addressing such subjects as accounting, advertising, promotion, and marketing.

Partnership

A partnership is one of two categories: general and limited.

- A general partnership is an association of at least two or more persons who co-own a business. Partnerships are formed when two or more persons agree to share ownership, management, profits, and liabilities of a business venture.

- A limited partnership is a partnership where only general partners may run the business, while limited partners cannot perform any management functions. However, limited partners may contribute capital, share in the profits, and are limited from liability. All partnerships must have at least one general partner, who remains personally liable for all debts and liabilities of the partnership, and any number of limited partners.

Personal Financial Statement (PFS)

Balance sheet showing personal assets and liabilities. A

personal financial statement shows how much net worth one has, while a tax return shows how much income one makes.

Personal Guaranty
A requirement by a franchisor or lender that the owner or borrower personally guarantee any debt to the franchisor or lender should the corporation default.

Product Format Franchise
The right to sell a product that does not represent all of the products that are sold.

Pro forma Financial Statement
A business owner's projected financial outlook for a company's operation in a financial format.

Protected Territory
A defined territory granted to the franchisee in the franchise agreement. The franchisor agrees not to open another comparable or similar franchise or company-owned operation within the franchisees protected territory.

Quality Control
The method by which the franchisor enforces the rules of operation set forth in the operations manual. Quality control can involve franchise representatives visiting franchisees.

Regional Development Agreement
A franchise right to develop or sell a person's franchise rights in a defined geographic area. A portion of the franchise fee is paid in advance for a certain number of franchise outlets.

Registration
Required in several states that the UFOC is submitted and approved by state authorities before franchises may be offered in

that state. The material contained in the registration may be more extensive.

Renewal

Renewal is the resigning or extension of a franchise agreement after the initial terms of the franchise agreement expires.

Royalty

The percentage of gross sales or some fixed fees paid to the franchisor on a periodic basis.

SBA

Small Business Association, located in Washington DC with regional offices. The SBA assists small businesses.

Service Mark

A mark used in the sale of a product or service which distinguishes them from the services of others. A trademark is associated with goods or products whereas service marks relate to services. Both have equal stature with the same protection under the law.

Sherman Antitrust Act

States that it is illegal to conspire or otherwise to restrain trade. Franchisees must be diligent and franchise agreements drafted to avoid exclusive allocated territories or price fixing.

Sole Proprietor

A business that is owned by one person. All income and losses generated by the business are treated as personal and will be filed along with the proprietor's regular tax returns.

Total Investment

The total amount of money estimated for the start-up of a franchise, including working capital, and subsequent additions to supplies and equipment necessary for a fully operational business.

Trade Secret

Knowledge in the possession of a company or entity that is commercially valuable, not generally known or readily ascertainable; and maintained in confidence by the trade secret owner or franchisor and by each franchisee to whom the information is disclosed.

Trademark

A tag or identifier by which individuals can differentiate your company or its services or products from those of other companies, services, and products which they come into contact.

Turnkey Financing

Financing for sale of a business which is structured so that the new owners need only "turns the key" in order to commence business.

Tying

Requiring the franchisee to purchase one product as a condition to the sale of another. Tying may be illegal if the products used in the franchise operation can be acquired from other sources at a lower price.

Uniform Commercial Code (UCC)

A code (law), which regulates commercial transactions. This code replaced the various state statutes covering mortgages, conditional sales, trust receipts, etc.

UFOC

An acronym for the Uniform Franchise Offering Circular. The disclosure documents that must be given to a franchise prior to selling a franchise.

Variable Cost

Operating costs that vary with the level of sales. Some costs such as labor may be semivariable.

Working Capital

Cash available for daily business operations.
(Current Assets - Current Liabilities = Working Capital)